The rewritten, up-to-date version of his best-selling book

All You Need To Know About
Commercial Awareness

CHRISTOPHER STOAKES

COMMERCIAL AWARENESS 2013/14

CW00953680

ΧΦΣ

British library cataloguing-in-publication data

A catalogue record for this book is available from the British Library.

Published by:

Christopher Stoakes Ltd

Marlowe House

Hale Road

Wendover

Bucks

HP22 6NE

ISBN: 978-0-9574946-1-9

First edition published February 2013.

Printed and bound in Great Britain.

Written by Christopher Stoakes; researched and edited by Viola Joseph.

Written, researched and edited at Scripto KT, Studio WO, Mews WO and Astoria DM.

© Christopher Stoakes 2013

What this book is about

This book is a completely revised, rewritten and up-to-date version of the best-selling guide *All You Need To Know About Commercial Awareness*.

It explains commercial awareness by looking at how businesses get and keep customers, why they need to compete, innovate and have a strategy, how they are funded, how they are organised and managed and the role of people in them. It explores the links between the private and public sectors, government and macro-economics. It shows that commercial awareness is a mindset that you can develop and provides tips and techniques for doing so.

Who this book is for

You are about to enter the world of work. Issue: your prospective employer says they expect applicants to have 'commercial awareness' or to be 'commercially aware'.

You know this means you need to have some understanding of business. But this will be your first proper job in business. So how can you know about business if you've never worked in it before? You can't.

This book solves that conundrum.

This book is for anyone facing that dilemma who needs to demonstrate commercial awareness in their role, but specifically for young people who are seeking their first employment or embarking on a career or are studying a vocational course where commercial awareness is a requirement or a help.

Above all it's required reading for any young person attending an interview who may need to demonstrate an understanding of what commercial awareness is.

Who this book is by

Chris Stoakes is the author of a number of best-selling books on the financial markets, law and business that students praise for making complex subjects easy to understand and enjoyable to read. By profession a lawyer, he has set up and run businesses of his own as well as with others. He has also been a management consultant, marketing director and financial journalist and has taught on an MBA. He has been the head of legal training and director of knowledge management at a top ten global law firm. Chris was a scholar at Charterhouse and Worcester College, Oxford where he read law.

CONTENTS

INTRODUCTION

I've written a book on commercial awareness before, called *All You Need To Know About Commercial Awareness*. It was popular but I wasn't completely happy with it. So I rewrote it. That edition was popular too. But it still didn't quite hit the mark for me. Yet I didn't know why. Then my editor spotted the reason.

It was too much about *how* to do certain things especially from the perspective of a professional adviser (I was originally a lawyer) and informed in part by the MBA I had taught on at Nottingham Law School and the work I had subsequently carried out as a management consultant.

Instead of talking about how to do certain things that might help to make you a successful professional the book needed to tell young people *what* the world of work is about in business terms so that they could get a job in it. My editor was right. It's what my readers wanted. And listening to your customers and potential customers is always good commercial awareness.

The other reason I've rewritten it is because the old versions were published by a business that managed to end up owing me a lot of money in unpaid royalties. Poor commercial awareness. So I took back the commercial rights and rewrote the book.

Here it is. I like it now. I hope you like it and it helps you in your career.

Your First Interview

You are about to enter the world of work. Issue: your prospective employer says they expect applicants to have 'commercial awareness' or to be 'commercially aware'. You know this means you need to have some understanding of business. But this will be your first proper job in business. So how can you know about business if you've never worked in it before? You can't.

In the old days it used to be enough if you were good at your job: say, a baker who made great bread. But that's not enough any more. On top of having the expertise needed to do your job (or role as it's now called) you need commercial awareness.

Commercial awareness is an understanding of why what you do is valuable, who finds it valuable, what they are prepared to pay for it and how it helps them in their own lives or roles.

So the baker needs to know which types of bread his customers like the best, how much it costs to make, how much he can charge and why and what hours he needs to stay open to maximise business. Being brilliant at making the bread itself is not enough. If he doesn't address these other issues somebody else whose bread isn't actually as good may sweep in and take his customers away. Maybe their bread is cheaper, maybe they are open very early in the morning and very late at night to accommodate customers' working and living routines. Maybe the bread that our baker thought was so great wasn't what they wanted. Maybe they wanted sliced bread to put in the freezer, not the crusty stuff he makes that goes hard the next day. You get the picture.

It's All About (And For) Us

The first thing to realise is that everything in life is about, and for, us. What we as humans want and need. The only reason there is business, there are jobs, is to provide something that people want. All human activity on the planet is designed to meet our needs.

And this is why man has always worked: providing others with what they want to satisfy his own needs and wants in turn. Whether it was growing crops or keeping animals, fishing, hunting, finding wood for fire or building huts for shelter, man has always worked. Initially he worked for himself and then, as society developed, for others by providing things that others wanted in return for money with which he in turn could buy whatever he needed.

And so it is today. Which is why you want a job. (So far I've been talking about man: by that I mean women too.)

You can begin to see that everyone is a customer, a consumer of goods and services. And everyone is also a supplier (assuming they are in work), providing goods or services that others want. These days we are all service providers with stakeholders we need to please.

And roles themselves are changing. You will no longer have a single job for life.

You are unlikely to work for just one employer. You need to understand your own personal value and how it changes. What is it you offer that other people want? What skills, what expertise? You will need to keep your skills relevant to the marketplace. You will have to redefine what you do at various points, maybe even retrain.

Coming back to your first interview, why is it that the prospective employer wants to recruit someone like you? What do they need you to do and be able to do? What skill set do you need to offer? Start to think like this and you are becoming commercially aware.

This book tells you all about commercial awareness. It tells you what you need to know. It tells you the terminology and what it means. It tells you how to demonstrate commercial awareness. You could say this book helps you to fake it.

In fact this book does more. It tells you what business is about so you can decide whether it's where you want to go with your life. In short this book could help you decide your future career.

Interest In The Way The World Works Commercially

So this book tells you all about all of this. But I hope it does more. I hope it sparks your interest in the way the world works commercially. I still go round supermarkets amazed at how much variety gets put on the shelves, picking up items to see which part of the world they are from. I still look up at the skies and marvel at how planes fly and airlines manage to make a profit from flying people around. I look at big buildings being built and wonder at how they are financed and which businesses will occupy them and why. If you have that sense of wonder then the world, and the world of business, will never be a boring place.

Interested? OK, let's go.

CHAPTER 1

BUSINESS, COMPETITION AND INNOVATION

Private sector – state – government – public sector – profit – loss –
insolvent – corporate – competition – innovation – efficiency – economies
of scale – volume discounts – cost of doing business – cost-per-unit –
market leaders – brands – reinvest – reward – shareholders – dynamic
environment

Anything provided by business is said to be provided by the **private sector**. This is because businesses are privately owned, that is, they are not owned by the state. By contrast, the **state** and **government** (whether central or local) is the **public sector**. State and government are the same. It's called public because in a sense we all own it and it is there for the benefit of all of us (it belongs to and is part of society).

SMEs And Big Business

The private sector is made up of businesses of different sizes. There are many, many SMEs as they are called (small and medium sized enterprises): newsagents, cafés, estate agents and so on, which are owned by the people who run them. They are all part of the private sector.

But there are also big businesses, big companies, some of which are household names like Sainsbury's and Tesco (supermarkets), Lloyd's and Barclays (banks), Shell and BP (oil companies), Marks & Spencer and Gap (clothing) and so on. These are all public companies (public here does not mean part of the public sector but listed on the London stock exchange so that anyone can buy shares in them – I'll explain this later). The biggest companies in the world are called multinational companies because they do business all over the world.

Making A Profit Or Going Bust

The purpose of these businesses is to provide goods and services that we want and to do so at a **profit**. Profit simply means that they earn more money from selling whatever they produce than they spend on providing it.

A business that makes a **loss** (its outgoings are greater than its income) will in due course run out of money and become **insolvent** (go bust) and cease to trade.

You may not realise this but there are businesses going bust every day and disappearing while other, new ones are created as inventors and entrepreneurs bring their ideas to market and see if they can make money out of them. Some businesses are taken over by others if they are failing or, in fact, if they are successful and provide the acquiring company with ready-made access to a new market it wasn't previously in. This is called mergers & acquisitions (M&A) and I'll talk about it later.

Competition And Innovation

All I want you to grasp for now is that the corporate landscape (**corporate** is another word for company) is forever changing as businesses with new ideas develop and businesses with old, past-it goods and services disappear. When I mentioned those household names above, I mentioned them in pairs for a specific reason: in business there is always **competition**. Sure, if you invent something new you can protect the idea from being copied (you can do this through intellectual property rights, which we'll explore later – intellectual because it's the product of people's mental creativity). But someone somewhere will always pop up to try to make and sell a better, different version of it.

Competition is at the heart of business. It leads to **innovation** (new ideas) and **efficiency** (cheaper ways of doing things). In business you can never stand still. If you do, your competitors will overtake you. This is why, in the main, businesses have to strive to get bigger and better. If they get bigger they can generate **economies of scale**. This means that because they are bigger, they buy more and can do so in bulk and get what are called **volume discounts**, so the **cost of doing business** is cheaper. Whatever they make if they make in greater quantity will have a lower **cost-per-unit** so they can sell it more cheaply and undercut their competitors, sell more of it and make more money. In this way they become the **market leaders** and their **brands** are more visible in the market.

At this point you may say: 'I'm not interested in things like profit. Profit is grubby. It's financial greed. I am an idealist and I want to spend my life doing things that are good, not doing things just to make money.' That's fair enough. But the reason for making profit is to **reinvest** in better products and services, to pay your employees and to **reward** the business backers (such as the **shareholders**, who own the business) for putting their money at risk by investing in the business to enable it to succeed.

The fact is that without businesses constantly innovating and finding efficiencies we would not have the goods and services we do nor would we be able to afford them. Think of all the amazing innovations that have happened over the last two hundred years that we now take for granted: electricity, light, film, television, recorded music, telephones, computers, mobile devices, cars, planes, etc, etc. When each of these was first created it was too expensive for ordinary people to benefit from. Think of the amazing innovation that Apple products represent and their affordability: quite extraordinary.

The sad fact is that the only other source of innovation is war: wars lead to technological innovation as people find more efficient ways of killing each other and better ways of protecting themselves from being killed.

So now I hope you are getting a sense of business being a very **dynamic environment** of constant innovation and change, which is why it can be an exciting place to work. You get innovation and change in all areas of human endeavour: in farming for instance (advance pesticides, crop resistance to disease); in government (delivering services and information on-line for instance); in education (case studies, storytelling, role play). But business is at the sharp end.

In the rest of this book we are going to explore how businesses get and keep customers, why they need a strategy, how they are funded, how they are organised and managed and, finally, the role of people – which is where we will come back to you and that interview. And once we have covered all of that you should be commercially aware. Then we'll finish with tips on how to maintain that commercial awareness.

How does that sound?

CHAPTER 2

THE QUEST FOR CUSTOMERS

Customers – professional service firms – clients – business development (BD) – marketing – selling – sales force – differentiation – unique selling proposition (USP) – price – quality – brand management – advertising – return on investment – media buying – business-to-consumer (B2C) – retail sales – mass marketing – Six Ps of Marketing – product – place – process – price – promotion – people – sales promotion – above-the-line marketing – below-the-line marketing – commoditisation – customer segmentation – customer value management – data mining – micromarketing – data warehouses – sales force automation – legacy systems – supply chain management – logistics – inventory management – margins – Wal-Mart – Disney – Volvo – Dell – mass customisation – longtail effect – time to market – product lifecycle – business-to-business (B2B) – Pareto Principle – client relationship management – request for particulars (RFP) – invitation to tender (ITT) – pitch – procurement – public procurement – value for money (VFM) – project management – reverse auction – competitor intelligence – industrial espionage

No business will survive unless it can find **customers** for its goods or services (incidentally, there is a business sector called **professional service firms** – accountancy, law, surveying and so on – where customers are always called **clients**; and these professional service providers are never called companies but are always called firms because they used to be partnerships, which I'll explain later).

Getting customers is called **business development (BD)**. Within BD, a distinction is usually drawn between **marketing** and **selling**. Selling is about getting an individual customer to buy something and for this reason some companies have a **sales force** – people who go round making sales on the company's behalf to customers.

Differentiation And USPs

Marketing is everything else that puts you in a position to make a sale. So marketing will include advertising, publicity, branding, customer research and segmentation, all of which I explain below. In order to get a customer to buy whatever it is you are offering, you have to differentiate yourself and/or your product in the market (product is increasingly used to mean either a good or a service even though originally it meant something you made (good) rather than something you did (service) so I will use it to mean both). **Differentiation** is critical to success and the way businesses achieve it is by developing something called a **USP** – their **unique selling proposition**. Your USP is what makes customers buy your product – it's what makes it different.

The usual distinction is drawn on grounds of **price** and **quality**: the higher the quality, the higher the price. Supermarkets stock branded goods made by well-known manufacturers but they also stock their own brand equivalents (often made by the same manufacturers but in the supermarket's name) which sell for less. In addition over recent years (because the recession meant people had less to spend) they introduced a further, cheaper level of own-label goods often called a value brand (usually called something like 'Simply' or 'Basics') in order to keep shoppers coming to their stores. This is very much about price versus quality.

Brands And Advertising

You can begin to see already the value of the brand. The biggest are consumer brands that are known globally like Coke, McDonald's, Nike and Starbucks. Brands are built on points of differentiation. These include service (the Ritz), innovation (Apple, Microsoft and most companies in the technology space), luxury (Louis Vuitton, Moët Hennessy, Rolls-Royce), environmental awareness (Body

Shop became successful for this), natural ingredients (Pret A Manger, Lush) and ethics (Co-operative Bank). **Brand management** is about how you communicate and project your goods and services to the market.

A brand will be supported in a number of ways, for instance through **advertising**. Advertising is an industry in its own right and is led by specialist advertising agencies. These are consultancies which develop advertising campaigns for big companies and place them on national television, billboards in cities, newspapers, local radio and the internet in a planned and coordinated way to gain maximum impact for the spend. It's why the leading newspaper for the advertising industry is called *Campaign*.

The ad agency will monitor and measure consumer response and increases in sales to see how successful the campaign has been and what the **return on investment** is (what the company has gained in sales as against the advertising spend).

Advertising agencies contain people who are expert at graphic design, copywriting (making up snappy slogans which is called advertising copy) and **media buying** (placing adverts in all of the different channels mentioned above). This is why advertising campaigns can cost tens of millions of pounds.

B2C: BUSINESS-TO-CONSUMER

Here we are focusing on **business-to-consumer (B2C)**, also known as **retail sales**. Advertising is about marketing to the mass of people out there (hence **mass marketing**) and the most visible aspect of B2C marketing is advertising.

Consumers are savvy buyers and it costs a lot of money to do any sort of marketing on sufficient scale and impact to reach us. Part of the role of advertising agencies is to do research into buyer behaviour and there are research agencies that collect this information and sell it to manufacturers and retailers (retailers are retail outlets: anything that has direct contact with consumers).

Supermarkets are amongst the most sophisticated operators in this area. Wonder why fresh fruit and vegetables are near the store entrance? It makes us feel good and healthy. Why is there a smell of freshly-baked bread around the bread counter? To make us buy the stuff. Next time you're in a supermarket, study the way the staff at the checkout treat you and what they say. Why have they been trained to do that?

Marketing experts talk about the **Six Ps of Marketing** as key ways in which organisations differentiate themselves. The six are **product** (what they sell), **place** (where they sell them), **process** (how they make them), **price** (what they charge), **promotion** (how they sell them) and **people** (who they are and what they are like to deal with).

Sales Promotion

Advertising is about brand awareness. There is a different discipline for making people actually buy at the point of sale (in a supermarket, for instance). **Sales promotion** is about point-of-sale promotion, things like special offers, twofers (two for the price of one), competitions and promotion of products at the checkout. Sales is a separate science in its own right. Many books have been written and academic studies conducted on how to maximise sales. The most famous book is *Getting To Yes* which is about negotiation. There are consultancies and advisers which specialise in turning people into great salesmen and saleswomen. If Sales is the sharp end of business development, Marketing embraces the wider aspects.

You can see now why advertising is called **above-the-line marketing**. By contrast sales promotion is **below-the-line marketing**.

Some people define marketing as meeting customer needs profitably. Others say that effective marketing makes selling unnecessary.

Mass Marketing, Customer Segmentation And Customer Value Management

In the old days B2C mass marketing was pretty indiscriminate. It was about selling the same thing to lots of people. This was immediately after World War Two in 1945 at a time when most people didn't have the things we take for granted now (cars, TVs, fridges, washing machines, dishwashers) and the ability to manufacture something in its millions (**commoditisation**) was itself novel. Now, however, the focus is on **customer segmentation** which is a way of breaking down your customer base to detect buying patterns.

Supermarkets collect a lot of data on what individual shoppers buy (e.g. through loyalty cards) and use this information to develop promotions and special offers. They analyse profiles of particular types of customer and their preferences. They now look at individuals in terms of their lifetime value to the business rather than just in terms of individual transactions. This approach is called **customer value management** (turning each interaction with a customer into an opportunity to learn more about, and sell more to, that customer). Every time you go into the supermarket you may spend only £20. But if you go there three times a week, that's £3,000 a year and over ten years that's £30,000. That's big business from just one customer.

Data Mining And Data Warehouses

There is a way of sifting through huge amounts of data like this using mathematical algorithms to detect patterns. It's called **data mining**. The US army uses it to help tanks identify enemy silhouettes on murky horizons through mapping previous enemy movements when visual and radar confirmation of identity aren't fool-proof. Banks use it to detect risk and default trends by customer type amongst portfolios of hundreds of thousands of loans for different customer types. Mail order retailers use it to segment customers by buying habits and patterns (known as **micromarketing**). Car manufacturers use **data warehouses** to store solutions to previous issues that will help them, for example, detect a problem on the production line and what to do about it in seconds (since any gap in car production can cost millions in lost units).

Sales Force Automation

Even the traditional door-to-door salesman has been turned into a superman with **sales force automation** which enables him (or her) with laptop and mobile to offer immediate customised order fulfilment. Sales force automation enables information about products and orders to be kept up-to-date in real time and made available at all contact points (sales force, call centre, local branch, head office, after-sales service, complaints) simultaneously giving the company a so-called 360-degree view of each customer. This means that whenever you call and whoever you speak to at a company, they can have instant access to your up-to-date consumer profile.

This, like data mining (inspecting data) and data warehousing (keeping it), is highly technology-enabled. But big businesses are hampered from doing this effectively by their **legacy systems** (previous generations of information technology) used to store existing data. Often it is laborious and expensive to make different technology platforms operate effectively together within the same business and to migrate data from old to new systems. Supplying big businesses with the technology to do these things is itself a big business.

However, this sort of information enables businesses to react quickly to changes in buying patterns. So, for example, US retailer Wal-Mart (which owns Asda in the UK) famously used this type of data in order to put babies' nappies (diapers in the States) alongside beer on its shelves, so boosting sales of both. This is because it saw that women often send their men out to buy diapers while they stay at home looking after baby; and men reward themselves for doing so by buying beer at the same time. So Wal-Mart increases sales of both by stocking them alongside each other.

Supply Chain Management

This sort of data informs **supply chain management** (also known as **logistics**). Ever wondered how supermarkets keep their shelves stocked at all times without having to have huge amounts of stock (called inventory) out back? It's because cashtill data tells them precisely how much they are selling of any item and how much they still have in stock (**inventory management**).

Supermarkets cannot afford to have gaps on their shelves: their **margins** (profit element) are so tight that any gap is potentially a lost sale. Equally they want to keep right quantities of stock: too much and their storage costs increase as does wastage through sell-by dates expiring.

Such sophisticated use of data and stock control means that **Wal-Mart** can move all of its stocks of, say, gloves from all over the States to the eastern seaboard overnight so that when snow hits the East coast the next day the demand for gloves can be met. Another example is **Disney**. Each Disney theme park trucks in vast quantities of hamburgers and beverages by night (usually via underground tunnels) in response to the previous day's aggregate cash till data logging sales of different items.

Supply chain management is an industry in its own right, involving shipping companies, airfreights and truck haulage. But it's also a science. It's no good having your manufacturing working at full capacity if it's simply creating inventory that needs to be stored somewhere and is ageing so may never be sold (all of which represents a cash investment). At the same time you need an optimal number of distribution hubs: too few and you need many more trucks making longer journeys, the return legs of which they will be travelling empty.

Estimating how many products to make to meet expected demand, taking into account seasonal fluctuations and the transportation time, can lead to massive over- or under-production which in turn can make a business go bust. It's mission-critical stuff.

Supply chain management brings together the processes linking marketing and sales with production, the physical facilities involved (factories, warehouses, trucks, ships and airfreight) and the technology that helps to plan, manage and predict customer demand. All these things involve trade-offs – between manufacturing flexibility and location, distribution cost and inventory holding.

Volvo And Dell

Swedish carmaker **Volvo** originally made cars with a wide array of specifications (extras and colour schemes) in the hope that most of them would find buyers. When it found its inventory of unsold cars was increasing it turned itself inside out.

Instead of making cars and then encouraging customers to buy them it refitted its showrooms so that customers could specify precisely what they wanted from hundreds of options. Only then would it make the car, effectively making it to order.

But customers are impatient. It had to re-engineer all of its manufacturing to be able to deliver the ordered car in a matter of a few weeks.

The same with **Dell** which famously only makes each computer in response to an order yet is able to deliver it within a few days.

Mass Customisation And The Longtail Effect

Both are examples of **mass customisation**: mass production but to meet individual preferences. A further example (fuelled by customer value management and internet retailers like Amazon and eBay) of 'mass markets of one' is the **longtail effect**. This term was coined by Chris Anderson, the founder of *Wired* magazine, to capture the idea that products with limited appeal can still be viable economically. The name comes from a typical demand graph which has a peak at one end where demand is high then tails off as demand declines.

Conventional thinking is that a manufacturer can only make money where demand is high. Take books. In the old days, books had to be printed in bulk (owing to the limits of printing presses) and sold in volume. Nowadays, print-on-demand (using digital printing) is viable for short print runs. If you imagine that Amazon is a bookshop with infinite shelf space, it actually makes more money from selling millions of different books in ones or twos than it does from a best-seller in much higher volume. That's the longtail effect.

Time To Market And Product Lifecycle

Two other big factors are **time to market** (how long it takes to invent a product, design, manufacture and market it and get it into stores) and **product lifecycle** (how long before a product goes out of date and is no longer attractive to consumers). Both are getting shorter and shorter so the pace of business is itself hotting up.

B2B: BUSINESS-TO-BUSINESS

All of this is reasonably visible to us. By contrast a lot of industry is **B2B** (**business-to-business**), businesses supplying other businesses which in turn may supply directly to the consumer. Two industries that create a huge number of knock-on businesses and jobs are car manufacture (e.g. Volvo, already mentioned) and defence. Think of all the components that make up a car: engine parts, lights, windscreen wipers, windscreens, steering wheel, seats and so on. The majority of these parts are bought in from other companies. In defence, think of all the technological advances to make warfare more efficient (I'm observing this, not advocating it) and you get the same idea. Just for us to be able to turn a light switch on at home or to stay warm in winter requires enormous power generation. Think of the equipment needed to do this. There will be manufacturers you have never heard of that make this stuff.

Pareto Principle

The same BD principles apply in B2B but instead of having to reach a mass market (people), businesses have to reach a smaller number of other businesses. If you make car windscreen wipers, it's pretty obvious that your customers will be a small number of global car manufacturers. For businesses in B2B something called the **Pareto Principle** generally applies, which is that 80% of your business comes from 20% of your customers and it's that 20% you need to focus on (the Pareto Principle applies in lots of other contexts too).

Client Relationship Management

One development of this is an emphasis on **client relationship management** (CRM) where business development is about focusing on a small number of your biggest customers, trying to get close by forging close contacts at different organisational levels, understanding customers' strategies and where the buying power lies.

In B2B you don't go for mass marketing. You generally have a much smaller number of customers (and if you are a professional service firm like a firm of accountants or lawyers, you call them clients).

Pitches For Business

Instead of trying to appeal to a mass of customers you acquire clients one at a time. Each one is usually a big organisation in its own right. It will draw up a long list of possible suppliers to meet a particular need. It will send out an **RFP** (**request for particulars**, also known as an **ITT – invitation to tender**) to each of them inviting them to submit a tender. A tender is basically a document pitching for the organisation's business, setting out what the supplier can do and at what cost (which is why it's often called a pitch document and the process is called a **pitch**). From these submissions the organisation will draw up a short list of say three or four, interview each one and decide which it wants to use.

Buying in goods and services in this way is called **procurement**. When governments and public bodies do it it is called **public procurement** and is usually subject to strict rules to ensure all suppliers are treated equally.

Cost is usually a critical factor. If the organisation can't pick between two suppliers it may ask each for its best and final fee offer and decide on price. The suppliers in question will seek to demonstrate why they offer the best **VFM** (**value for money** – an important term in the commercial world). Another major factor may be how good a supplier is at **project management** (organising and running a piece of work) using methodologies like Prince 2 and Gantt charts (timelines showing critical paths and dependencies).

Some organisations will appoint a panel of suppliers to provide a service and then choose between them for each piece of work by deciding on price: the supplier bidding the lowest price will win that piece of work (this is known as a **reverse auction**). Often this is done by e-auction where each bidder submits a quote by email.

Which Products To Offer?

You can begin to see that businesses of all types are in competition for customers or clients. It's this fostering of competition that leads to innovation and efficiency (the same or better good or service at lower cost and/or more rapid delivery). It follows that a business needs to think carefully about what goods or products to offer to the market and how best to offer them to make them distinctive. If everyone did the same thing no one would be successful.

So businesses have to consider what their competitors are doing and what they can do to be different and then major on it. Knowing what your competitors are doing (**competitor intelligence**) is crucial but if businesses step over the line of the law it's known as **industrial espionage** and they can end up in court.

In a sense business is a race and the one who gets there quickest wins. The choices you make over which products to offer, to whom and at what price (elements of marketing mentioned above) are critical.

In order to decide these you need to know the direction in which you are trying to go. This is called strategy and we look at it next.

CHAPTER 3

A SENSE OF DIRECTION

Strategy – vision – mission – corporate culture – McKinsey – 7-S
Framework – industry sectors – conglomerates – diversified businesses –
management consultants – business schools – Harvard – MBA –
business models – SWOT analysis – strengths – weaknesses –
opportunities – threats – Porter's Five Forces – competitors – buyers –
suppliers – new entrants – substitutes – Boston Consulting Group – dog –
divest – cash cow – stars – question marks – external business
environment – PESTL – technological innovation – convergence of
platforms – convergence of content – distributed or networked data –
cloud – monetise – channels to market – bricks 'n' clicks – barriers to
entry –disruptive technology – disintermediation – secular trends – step
changes – paradigm shifts – consumerism – globalisation – multinational
companies (MNCs) – World Trade Organisation – Fairtrade – strategic
alliances – joint ventures – international trade – parallel imports – grey
markets – transfer pricing – knowledge economy – Peter Drucker –
knowledge workers – knowledge management – intellectual property –
trademarks – copyright – patents – portfolio – intellectual property rights
(IPR) – manufacturing economy – service economy – corporate
responsibility – stakeholders – carbon footprint – corporate governance

The most successful businesses have a sense of direction, of momentum. They know what makes them different, what their USP is and this helps them set a course or direction which will enable them to succeed. This is called strategy.

Strategy, Vision And Mission

A **strategy** is simply a set of business objectives and a plan for how to achieve them. You may hear business leaders talk about having a **vision** for their business. Often it can be boiled down to a slogan or an aspiration. NASA, the American space programme, famously had a vision to *put a man on the Moon* by the end of the 1960s. They achieved it in 1969. British Airways once upon a time said it was *the world's favourite airline*. General Electric after World War Two had a vision to put a *refrigerator (fridge) in every American home*. Bill Gates, founder of Microsoft, had a vision to put *a computer in every home* (this was at a time when computers were only used in business and the received wisdom was that the world would be run by a small number of huge computers – so Gates's vision was revolutionary). Steve Jobs's vision was to create machines that were so beautiful they were works of art and so simple that you knew intuitively how to use them.

But not all businesses have such straightforward and striking visions or strategies. It's very difficult to encapsulate what a business is or does that makes it different – and then to match that aspiration with reality. But if an organisation can pinpoint what makes it different or can clarify its purpose or mission (another term you hear in this context) then it's easier for everyone in the business to pull together with a collective and shared sense of purpose. **Mission** is often described as the route map to achieving the vision. Mission is the purpose. By pursuing your purpose you realise (make real, achieve) your vision.

Sometimes what makes a business different is its **corporate culture** – what it feels like to work there and why customers keep coming back. Culture was once defined by the head of **McKinsey**, a famous management consultancy, as 'the way we do things round here'. In fact McKinsey developed the **7-S Framework** which pinpoints seven factors (each beginning helpfully with an S) that help make organisations different. The seven are: structure, systems, style, skills, staff, shared values (= culture) and strategy.

Industry Sectors

The very first strategic decision a business has to take is what business it's in. The principal **industry sectors** include:

- Agriculture (farming and food production)
- Extractive industries (oil, gas, coal, minerals)
- Construction (buildings, roads, airports, ports)

- Transport (including shipping)
- Manufacturing (probably the biggest) which has within it:
    - Automotive (cars)
    - Aviation (planes) and
    - Defence (armaments)
- Retail (shops)
- Technology
- Financial services (banking, insurance and wealth management)
- Healthcare (hospitals, doctors)
- Pharmaceuticals (drugs)
- Education and training
- Professional services (such as accountancy, advertising, actuarial, law, management consulting, surveying)
- Hospitality (tourism, holidays, hotels, restaurants, casinos)
- Sports
- Arts and media (including film, TV, newspapers and publishing)

Businesses that do the same or a similar thing are said to belong to the same sector or industry and are likely to be competitors. Businesses that straddle sectors (are active in more than one) are called **conglomerates**. They do this to diversify (reduce) the risk of being in just one and so are also called **diversified businesses**.

You can see from this list that the sectors fall into three: primary (extraction of natural resources including oil, minerals and agriculture); secondary (conversion of natural resources into products through manufacturing) and tertiary (the services sector ranging from insurance to tourism). Some argue that there is a fourth (quaternary) sector which is about the exploitation of know-how: information, research and education.

Business Schools And Business Models

There is a whole industry of **management consultants** that advises businesses on strategy (McKinsey, quoted above, is one of many global consultancies). **Business schools** exist to teach it (the most famous is **Harvard** in the States) and associated issues to do with running organisations. People who go to business school – they tend to be people in their 30s and 40s with experience of business – get a qualification called an **MBA** (Master of Business Administration). Most business leaders have an MBA, as do the management consultants that advise them, such as McKinsey.

Business schools and the professors (academics) in them devise and teach **business models** (ways of encapsulating ideas in short words or pictures) which help people leading businesses to focus on the factors that will make them successful. So, for example, regardless of which business you're in, there will be certain factors that will determine your success.

There are many, many models that help businesses strategise (the magazine *Harvard Business Review* is where management academics publish their latest research and theories) but the following are examples of the most famous.

SWOT

The simplest and most well-known is the **SWOT analysis**. SWOT stands for **strengths**, **weaknesses**, **opportunities** and **threats**.

This encourages an organisation to look internally (within) at what's good about it (strengths) and where it is vulnerable (weaknesses) and to look externally (outside) at the opportunities (to gain new customers or enter new markets) and the threats (competitors or changes in the external environment).

Critics say this can be too subjective and simplistic an assessment. But it is quick to do and to repeat on a regular basis and can be applied at any level in a business. So a supermarket can apply SWOT to its entire business or to an individual store.

Porter's Five Forces

Michael Porter, a management academic, studied many businesses and realised that common forces influence their success. His model, **Porter's Five Forces**, identifies them as:

- Your industry **competitors**,
- Who your **buyers** (customers) are (they will try to force down the price at which they buy from you) and
- Your **suppliers** (they will try to force up the price at which they sell the raw commodities you need to produce finished goods).

So far so obvious. But then he hit upon two others that businesses need to be mindful of. These are:

- **New entrants** – new competitors who will enter your market because they spot rich pickings (at your expense) and
- **Substitutes** – people who will decide they can do without your product because they can do it themselves or find alternatives.

If you're seeking a job at a company, you should think about its business in these terms. Its top people certainly will. Supermarkets moving into financial services are new entrants. People who sell their house by putting a For Sale sign outside rather than going to an estate agent are substitutes.

BCG Product Matrix

Another famous business model was created by **Boston Consulting Group** (like McKinsey, a management consultancy) and it's called the BCG Product or Growth-Share Matrix. Most businesses have more than one product or service line and the BCG model helps them work out which to invest in. The two key factors are: how much market share do you have (as against your competitors); and is that market fast-growing or is it mature?

- Mature markets necessarily do not offer much further growth. So if you have a *small share* of a *mature market*, there's no point in focusing much effort there. In fact BCG call it a **dog** and say you should get rid of it (**divest**).

- But if you have a *big share* of a *mature market*, BCG call this a **cash cow** (because it makes good money and provides a steady income flow) and they say you should use this to generate cash to invest in fast-growing markets.

- If you have a *big share* of a *fast-growing market* you need to focus your efforts (and cash) here. These are what BCG call **stars**.

- Finally there are *fast-growing markets* in which you have a *small share* (maybe because you've held back because you're not sure whether they are going to turn into big markets worth the effort). BCG call these **question marks** – you need to watch them closely to see how they develop and whether to invest fully.

External Environment

A business cannot devise a strategy in a vacuum. It has to think about the world around it and how that is changing (one of the purposes of strategy is to make businesses light on their feet, to make them focus on the **external business environment** and how that is shaping the future from the present and what that means for them).

So, for example, the biggest forces changing our world can be grouped under the headings political, economic, social, technological and legal (known amongst management experts as **PESTL**). At any one time one or more of these will be uppermost in shaping your markets. For example, when China opened up internationally, the greatest factor was political. But as a new middle class emerged it was social. For the world as a whole, over the past thirty years it has been technological.

Examples Of Technological Change

We've already looked at some aspects of **technological innovation**. This has seen a **convergence of platforms** as television, computers, video games, internet access and mobile phones all started to be provided by the same tablet device, and a **convergence of content**, as films, music, television, video games and news all started to be streamed to the same device. Traditional ways of storing and selling data (records, CDs, DVDs) have died and been replaced by **distributed or networked data** where applications don't reside on your device but together with content are stored in the computing **cloud** and are instantly accessible whenever and wherever you want. The key is how to **monetise** these innovations (turn them into money) which has led to new business models (new ways of doing business) such as subscription services and streamed services that survive on advertising revenue.

The internet has offered businesses new **channels to market** (ways of reaching their customers) so that it's common for retailers to have both actual, physical shops as well as online portals (a strategy known as **bricks 'n' clicks**). Business leaders have to be aware all the time of how these factors will affect their business and whether these will lower **barriers to entry** allowing more competitors in. Technology which has a fundamental and immediate impact is called **disruptive technology** – it changes the competitive landscape and channels to market overnight.

The web is also allowing **disintermediation** – the by-passing – of conventional businesses. Traditional 'publishers' ranging from newspapers to radio stations and record companies are being disintermediated.

For instance, record companies have lost control of the physical product of recorded music through downloading and are being by-passed by musicians who are seeking an audience directly through YouTube and MySpace.

Book publishers are also finding that authors are publishing themselves through print-on-demand and ebooks. Wikipedia, the free on-line encyclopaedia, is hitting traditional encyclopaedia publishers hard.

It's thought that the last newspaper will cease publication around 2040. Already some are available on-line, free, and aren't produced in hard-copy form. This by-passing effect is happening in the wider world as a result of the web, allowing blogging and podcasting. People are no longer passive consumers of information. They are active in its creation. Wikis (web pages that allow anyone to log into them and change them) allow collaboration and the sharing of knowledge on a mass scale with few attendant costs.

Secular Trends And Paradigm Shifts

There are other big trends (often called **secular trends**) shaping our future (where these lead to significant change they are called **step changes** or **paradigm shifts**). For example, we've talked about supermarkets which are symbolic of the rise of **consumerism**, the idea that everyone is a buyer whose needs are there to be addressed. Shopping used to be a way of buying the boring things needed to live. But with the explosion in fashion, food and entertainment shopping malls are now places where people go for a day out. Now it's a leisure activity. Look how many shops have cafés and even restaurants. Look at opening hours. In the old pre-consumer days, shops would have early closing days (usually Wednesdays and Saturdays) and wouldn't open at all on Sunday (that was for going to church). Now they are open every day and some are 24/7.

Retail Revolution

As a result, the world has gone retail. The consumer is king and whoever controls access to the consumer is market-dominant. And that is retailers. So important is the retail space that publishers have to pay to get their books in window displays. If manufacturers don't deliver goods in packaging that fits directly on supermarkets' shelves, those goods are turned away. So strong is the retail channel to market that supermarkets drive hard bargains with suppliers and require them to manufacture own-label goods (i.e. bearing the supermarket's logo, not the manufacturer's). Look at how many supermarkets have gone into lending, insurance, investment and other financial services. Incredible that the humble cornershop is now a bank.

Even the basics of selling groceries have changed: because people travel they have much wider tastes and want greater and more exotic choice. They expect food to be fresh and available all-year round – just imagine the impact on a supermarket's supply chain: how quickly food needs to get to the shops and from how far afield. With online shopping and home deliveries, customers don't even have to come to the store.

If we do go to the store they've even got us doing their job for them – all in the name of choice! In the days of the corner shop, the man behind the counter got what you wanted down from the shelves and wrapped it for you. Now we do that; we push our trolley round, fill it ourselves, queue at the cashtill, put our purchases in bags and take them out to the car. In supermarkets that have automated tills you can do the checkout staff's job yourself. All of this saves supermarkets huge amounts of money. Soon they'll have us stacking the shelves….

Globalisation

Another big business trend is **globalisation**: the idea that the world is becoming a smaller place and we will all end up buying the same products and services. As the bank HSBC put it in its advertising, being global but thinking local. Major companies do a lot of business outside their home country, in search of new markets and more consumers. That's why they are often called **multinational companies** or **MNCs**.

The most obvious examples are those companies I've mentioned before whose brands are known the world over. Coke. Nike. Louis Vuitton. Looks can be deceptive. Car manufacturing is a global industry with almost 150 countries exporting car parts, which is why cars built by Ford in the US now have a higher proportion of foreign-made components than cars made by Toyota in the US, making Toyota's arguably more 'American' – whatever that means.

Competing For World Trade

As you can imagine, there's a lot of politics involved in this, from people who object to the homogenisation of life and protest against globalisation, to those who see that until the world is a level playing field, smaller exporting countries (often developing nations) will be crushed by larger ones (hence the role of the **World Trade Organisation** and movements like **Fairtrade**), and environmentalists who see big oil companies as wreckers of natural habitats and supermarkets as polluters (because they fly produce in overnight from far-flung corners of the world enabling consumers to get year-long access to produce that used to be seasonal).

Strategic Alliances And Joint Ventures

Global markets can be risky for businesses. They require enormous investment in brand and marketing to get any payback and raise their own issues for businesses. One way of expanding – especially overseas – is by entering into **strategic alliances** and **joint ventures** with local companies to exploit new markets together, sharing information and expenses and developing joint opportunities. At its grandest, a new company (NewCo, as it's often codenamed before being launched with a proper name) may be created (owned by the joint venture parties) which then undertakes a whole new business, with the two joint owners contributing capital, know-how and people.

International trade (as it's called) has its own issues. For example, **parallel imports** can occur where importers bring goods into a country other than directly from the manufacturer. **Grey markets** occur where goods are sold outside official import channels. There are rules against **transfer pricing** where a manufacturer seeks to gain tax advantages by selling goods to associated companies in other countries at artificial prices.

The Knowledge Economy

Another secular trend in business is the move towards service economies and away from manufacturing. Linked to it is the idea, even in manufacturing, that what a business knows (for instance about its customers – see above) is the most important component of its success. This is the idea of the **knowledge economy**, a term invented by **Peter Drucker**, possibly the greatest management thinker of the twentieth century (he was born in 1909 and died in 2005).

The pillars of capitalism used to be money (capital), the means of production (equipment) and an abundance of cheap labour (employees). But nowadays people recognise that technology has reduced the cost of production and that competitive advantage depends not on how much you make and at what price but on what you know. Your employees are no longer just muscle and brawn needed to operate machines; they are now **knowledge workers**.

Take something as basic as getting coal or oil out of the ground: what matters is knowing where to dig or drill. The same with farming: knowing about soil and crop rotation is what makes the difference. And these are all examples of primary industries (where the skills involved were regarded as basic and involved simple commodities found in the ground or earth).

Now a business's most important assets have feet – and they walk out of the door every evening. Companies recognise that what their employees carry round in their heads is critical to the business. If what matters is what you know, it follows that businesses need to try to record and store this information and make it available organisation-wide. This is called **knowledge management.** Businesses now have chief information officers (CIOs) and know-how managers to capture and organise the business's knowledge and focus on how they record, store and share it.

Intellectual Property Rights

This is related to **intellectual property** which includes **trademarks** (to protect brands), **copyright** (for instance my copyright in this book as its author) and **patents** (which protect inventions). Big companies will have a **portfolio** of patents and many registered trademarks. These collections of patents and trademarks are referred to collectively as **intellectual property rights** (**IPR**). A company's IP can be its single most important asset. It's the licence fees for using Windows that have made Bill Gates as rich as he is. As the developed world becomes less of a **manufacturing economy** and more of a **service economy**, what a company knows becomes its biggest source of competitive advantage.

Being A Good Corporate Citizen

Another big theme in business is that of **corporate responsibility**, also known as corporate citizenship. It's the idea that a business is not there just to make money but owes a duty to its **stakeholders**, such as its employees and their families, pensioners (past employees), its local community and its customers, as well as its owners. It owes a duty to the environment, not to pollute it (hence the emphasis on a business's **carbon footprint** meaning the amount of energy it consumes and carbon it produces as a result). This also extends to encouraging a diverse workforce which is representative of society in terms of gender, religion and ethnicity. A specific aspect of this is **corporate governance** which is about how a business is made accountable to its owners and stakeholders.

So far I've been using the terms business and company interchangeably. Now we need to look in more detail at who those owners are and the forms that businesses can take.

CHAPTER 4

BUSINESS FORMATS

Sole trader – trading name – partnership – unincorporated businesses – unlimited liability – incorporate – company – entrepreneurs – professional partnerships – firms – joint and several liability – limited liability partnerships – private companies – small and medium sized businesses (SMEs) – public companies – stock exchange – go public – listing – flotation – initial public offering (IPO) – venture capital – mergers & acquisitions (M&A) – takeover – bidder – target – premium – quoted price – subsidiary – parent – group – share-for-share exchange – hostile bids – corporate finance – competition laws – management buy out (MBO) – FTSE 100 – franchising – McDonald's

We've looked at what industry and sector a business may be in, and the purpose behind strategy. Now we need to look at what form a business can take.

Unincorporated Businesses

You can start up in business on your own, working for yourself. This is called being a **sole trader**. You can use your own name (C Stoakes) or devise a **trading name** (Brightwash Launderette). Plumbers, market stall-holders, authors, decorators – these tend to be self-employed people who work on their own for themselves. If two or more people work together they may decide to be in **partnership** together, splitting the profit between them. All of these are called **unincorporated businesses**.

The problem with all of these is that the individuals involved are liable for the debts of the business. If the business goes bust with big liabilities, then they can end up personally bankrupt too. This is called **unlimited liability**.

Companies (Incorporated Businesses)

This is why most businesses **incorporate** (become companies). A **company** has directors who run it and shareholders who own it (in small businesses the two tend to be the same; you can have a company with one director and one shareholder where they are the same person).

But, crucially, neither the directors nor shareholders are liable for the company's debts. If it goes bust they don't. This enables businesses to take risks. I don't mean gambling risks but risks in terms of developing new products that might not find a market. Any innovation is risky and many turn out not to work at all or to be too complex or expensive or unappealing to be attractive to customers. But it's still important that they are able to be put to the test. Companies enable people to do that.

People who regularly set up new businesses are called **entrepreneurs**. Even the most successful entrepreneur will usually have had at least one business disaster before they find success. That's why limited liability can be so important.

Professional Partnerships

Traditionally, some types of business – mainly involving professionally qualified people such as solicitors and accountants – were partnerships. As these **professional partnerships** (called **firms**) got bigger they behaved more like companies (a major law or accounting firm can have over a thousand partners). So it was no longer appropriate that each partner could be liable for the entire business – each partner being liable for everything is called **joint and several liability** since the partners are liable together (jointly) and on their own (severally).

26

For this reason large partnerships are nowadays often **limited liability partnerships** (LLPs) which have the same benefit as companies of protecting individual partners from the debts of the business as a whole.

Private And Public Companies

Companies generally start off as **private companies** with a small number of shareholders who tend to be individuals.

They are called private because they tend to be owned by a small number of people. Most **SMEs (small and medium sized enterprises)** are private companies. They have the word 'Limited' or 'Ltd' at the end of their name. This warns people who trade with them that they have limited liability.

A company that becomes very successful may decide to become a public company. **Public companies** have their shares listed on a **stock exchange** (any country with a financial centre usually has a stock exchange at the heart of it) which means their shares can be bought and sold by the public (hence the term 'public company'). In the UK they tend to have the letters PLC (public limited company) after their name.

Reasons For Going Public

Why would a company **go public**, which is also known as a **listing**, **flotation** or **initial public offering (IPO)**? There are three main reasons.

The first is that it enables the founders of a company to take some money out without having to sell the business in its entirety. Since people who start businesses often have to borrow a lot of money to do so, even mortgaging their house, it follows that being able to get some cash out is a good thing, even if it's just to pay off those debts.

Second, there may be other investors who want to get their money out too, investors who've provided **venture capital**. Venture capitalists provide capital (money) that is at risk (venture as in 'adventure'). In other words their business is investing in small businesses that may or may not be successful. On average, two out of every three businesses goes bust. So they need to sell their shares in those that are successful to make up for those that aren't.

Third, the company may need additional capital to expand. By going public it can raise this additional money to invest in the business. It issues additional shares to people who want to buy them and uses the money they pay for those shares to put into the business.

M&A

I talked earlier about the fact that businesses can never stand still, that if they do their competitors will overtake them, which is why businesses strive to get bigger and better because then they can generate economies of scale.

One way of expanding is through taking another business over. When public companies take each other over this is called **M&A** which stands for **mergers & acquisitions**.

In a **takeover** one company (the **bidder**) makes an offer to buy all the shares in another company (the **target**) for a stated price which is usually at a **premium** to (higher than) the target's **quoted price** (the price its shares are trading at on the stock exchange).

The premium is designed to encourage the target's shareholders to sell their shares in the target to the bidder. If more than half of them do, the target will become a **subsidiary** of the bidder (which will be its **parent** company) and therefore part of the bidder's **group** (short for group of companies).

Bidders usually offer their own shares as payment to the target's shareholders (known as a **share-for-share exchange**) so the target's shareholders become shareholders in the bidder and therefore continue to share indirectly in the fortunes of their former company, the target. Offering shares is cheaper for the bidder than if it had to raise cash to pay the target's shareholders in money instead.

Hostile Bids

Takeovers are generally used by big, strong companies to take over smaller, weaker ones, either to increase their market share in one market or to move into a new market but without having to start from scratch with a start-up.

Sometimes these bids can become acrimonious (and are known as **hostile bids**) if the target's directors reject the bid, especially if the bidder is saying it can do a better job of managing the target's business (which generally means the target's management will lose their jobs if the bid is successful).

Corporate Finance

Listing on an exchange raises money for a business, and taking another company over in an M&A deal sometimes requires funding (for instance, if the target's shareholders want cash instead of shares in the bidder).

So the two activities are often described as **corporate finance**. It's about companies (corporate) and money (finance). Bankers and lawyers who advise companies on listings and M&A will often say they do corporate finance.

Anti-Monopoly Law

If a bid is likely to create a dominant or near-monopoly position in a market then national and EU competition authorities (called anti-trust in the US from the time when companies coming together to form cartels were called trusts) may block the bid. Or they may impose conditions if it is successful, for instance requiring the combined bidder-target business to sell off some of its assets to reduce its dominance. So, two banks joining together may be required to sell off (divest) bank branches to avoid too much of a concentration in geographical areas.

The reason for these **competition laws** is that monopolies are bad for consumers: they restrict choice and enable businesses to raise their prices if there are no, or few, other businesses providing the same goods or services.

Management Buy Outs

A successful bidder may sell off bits of the acquired business it doesn't want, often to the management team running that business. This is called an **MBO** or **management buy out**. The managers won't have the money to buy the business. Instead they may seek venture capital funding and in return give shares in the business they are buying to the venture capital provider.

FTSE 100

In this way you can begin to see that companies begin, expand, acquire, wane and even die. Some can be around for two hundred years, others for less than twenty.

You might think that big businesses stay big and don't change much. In fact companies are forever taking each other over and restructuring themselves, spinning off non-core assets in MBOs for instance. In this way old, established names do disappear. It is this dynamic corporate landscape that keeps business innovative and competitive.

The **FTSE 100** is the index of the hundred biggest public companies in the UK by market capitalisation (FT stands for the *Financial Times*, the newspaper which publishes the index, and SE for the London Stock Exchange which compiles it) and over any given ten-year period about half of the companies in it drop out – they are taken over (and their name disappears) or they shrink and fall outside it.

Going back to Chapter 1, this is because of the forces of competition and innovation.

Franchising

Franchising is not a business format as such (it can be done by sole traders, partnerships and companies). But it is a highly effective method of building a brand.

Businesses, especially B2C, need to establish themselves in consumers' minds but at the same time usually lack the money to do so. Franchising is a clever business format that addresses both these issues. Let's say you create a new style of American diner for the UK market. You open an outlet in London. It's successful so you open another two. You want to repeat it across the UK as quickly as possible to build up the brand. But you can't afford to do it all yourself in one go.

So, instead you franchise the brand: you get other people to set up outlets – which you help them find, but they pay for – and you provide them with the logo, the diner layout, the décor, the staff uniforms, the menus, the recipes, ingredients and the training. In return they pay you a fee and a proportion of their profits. So, instead of having three diners in London there are instead, and almost immediately, ten across the country. This market penetration lodges the name in consumers' minds and leads to far more customers-per-diner than your three on their own could have generated. The rate of growth is exponential (the rate is itself accelerating). So everyone benefits: you and your franchisees.

McDonald's – Itself A Franchise

McDonald's is the most famous franchise. In fact Ray Kroc, who created the hamburger chain, himself franchised the idea from the two McDonald brothers who were cattle ranchers, had a beefburger café on their ranch but weren't interested in opening more. The famous arches logo was their ranch's insignia.

Pizza Express and Toni & Guy are just two high street names that have expanded through franchising outlets.

It isn't just franchisors who can get rich through franchising. McDonald's has made many people round the world millionaires through enabling them to become master franchisees (having more than one outlet and sub-franchising) in new markets.

A major reason for building a brand through franchising is capital (money). A franchise doesn't need the founder to put up as much capital to expand the business. Why this is significant we'll see in the next chapter.

CHAPTER 5

MONEY AND BUSINESS (1):

DEBT AND EQUITY

Debt – equity – capital – income – lender – loan – borrower – interest – principal – share – risk capital – share buybacks – dividends – compound interest – tax deductible – servicing debt – revolver – term loan – bullet – credit approval – due diligence – completion – drawdown – conditions precedent – legal opinions – certificates – credit analysis – security – charge – defaults – fixed – floating – enforce its security – guarantees – operating company – holding company – parent company guarantee – comfort letter – debenture – syndicated loan – acquisition finance – leveraged buy out (LBO) – highly geared – mezzanine finance – asset finance – finance leasing – hire purchase – conditional sale – bond – completion bond – international capital markets – cost of borrowing – tradable debt securities – debt issuance – issuer – fixed income bond – floating rate notes – basis points – high yield bonds – equity funding – preference shares – ordinary shareholders – warrants – convertible bonds – insurance – premium – self-insurance – hedging – derivatives – interest-rate swap – unwind – currency swap – option – forward – future

There are only two types of capital: **debt** and **equity**. Debt is money that is borrowed. Equity is money that is invested. The term **capital** applies to money that is used to fund an asset such as a business. You would use capital to buy a car but not to buy your groceries. You would buy your groceries out of **income** (see next chapter).

Debt

A provider of debt is called a **lender**. Money that is lent is called a **loan**. The **borrower** will pay for the use of the money over the life of the loan by paying **interest**.

The loan ends when the borrower repays the amount borrowed, called the **principal** (short for principal amount).

Interest is quoted as a percentage of the loan paid annually. If you lend me £100 at 5% interest, I pay you £5 each year for the use of the money over the life of the loan until I pay it back. Let's say I pay half back so I still owe you £50. I would continue to pay interest at 5% but on £50 that would be £2.50 a year.

Equity

Equity is money that is invested in a business (specifically a company) by shareholders. In return for putting money into the business they get a **share** in the business (which is why they are called shareholders). If four people set up a company together and they are equal shareholders, each will own 25% of the company. But if the company goes bust they lose their entire investment. This is why equity is also called **risk capital**.

Equity is not like debt, for two reasons.

First, it isn't repaid (unlike a loan). A shareholder does not provide equity for a limited time and then expect to get it back. Instead the shareholder hopes the company will do well and grow, in which case the shareholder's share in the company will itself grow in value. In due course the shareholder may sell his or her share to someone who will pay more for it than the original investment, reflecting the growth in the value of the business. This is what the venture capitalists (last chapter) do. Their business is investing in small, fast-growing companies. (This doesn't mean that a company will never pay back the equity to a shareholder: sometimes companies do **share buybacks** where they do exactly that; but it is unusual.)

Second, shareholders don't receive interest on the amount invested. Instead they hope to receive **dividends**. But this will depend on how well the business is doing. A company will only pay a dividend to shareholders if it has made a profit (see the next chapter) and if it can spare the money (that is, it doesn't need the money for cash flow purposes – again see the next chapter).

So shareholders hope to get two things: capital growth (the business will be a success and their share in it will go up in value correspondingly); and dividends.

You've probably heard home owners talk about the equity they have in a house. They mean what is left once the house is sold and the debt (the mortgage) paid off: in other words, the bit they own – the value in the house that is theirs. You can see now why the term 'equity' applies there too.

Why Businesses Like Debt

As individuals we generally try not to borrow too much. We will take out a mortgage (a loan that enables you to buy a flat or a house) because (1) we need a place to live, (2) property tends to increase in value over time and (3) mortgages are long-term loans often for as long as twenty-five years. So mortgages are OK.

By contrast, credit cards charge high rates of interest on any balance that you fail to pay off at the end of the month. Soon you can be paying interest on interest (known as **compound interest**) and getting deeply into debt. So as individuals we should be suspicious of debt.

However, credit cards are good for enabling you to buy something expensive, like a holiday, which is just too much for you to buy all-in-one-go from one month's salary or income. In short, credit cards help with cash flow.

Interest Is Tax-Deductible...

Businesses look at debt entirely differently. For them debt is good, and that is because the interest they pay on debt is **tax deductible**. Everyone who earns money pays tax. Individuals pay income tax. Companies pay corporation tax. But companies only pay tax on their profits. And they deduct from their income their costs of doing business to arrive at what their profit is. One of those costs is paying interest on loans known as **servicing debt**. (As individuals we aren't allowed to deduct interest on debt from our taxable income.)

... But Dividends Are Paid Out Of Taxed Income

By contrast, dividends on shares are paid out of taxed income. They are not tax-deductible. This makes equity more expensive for companies than debt, so they tend to have a high proportion of debt in their capital base. But remember that companies don't have to pay dividends even if they make profits – they may decide to reinvest the profit in the business, whereas they always have to pay the interest due on their debt.

Another reason why companies like to borrow as much as they can is that the more money you have available to you, the quicker you can grow, outflank your competitors and achieve your strategy. A business starved of investment cannot expand as quickly as one that has access to money – and risks being overtaken by richer competitors.

DEBT: LOAN-BASED FUNDING

There are different types of loan. For example:

- A **revolver** (or revolving loan facility) is like an overdraft. With an overdraft there is a maximum up to which you can borrow, but whatever you pay back you can borrow again. So if I have an overdraft facility of £100 at the bank, I can borrow, say, £70, repay £50 and still borrow a further £80. Corporate overdrafts are called revolving loans or revolvers.

- A **term loan** is a loan for a fixed period. If it is a **bullet**, the company repays the principal all in one go at the end (unlike, say, a repayment mortgage where your monthly payments include interest and a bit of principal so that by the end of the mortgage you've paid off all the principal as well as the interest on it).

Before lending, a bank will go through its internal **credit approval** process, involving **due diligence** (examining the company's financial standing). Once the loan agreement has been negotiated and signed (this is called **completion**) the company can actually get the money (called **drawdown**) provided it satisfies some **conditions precedent** (obtains **legal opinions** and **certificates** confirming the documents are duly signed and the borrower is legally capable of borrowing).

Security

As part of its **credit analysis** the lending bank may seek **security** – that is, a legal mechanism (often called a **charge**) that allows the bank to seize and sell the company's assets if the company **defaults** (fails to repay interest or principal).

A charge may be **fixed** (over particular assets) or **floating** (which allows the company to deal with those assets). If the bank sells assets it is said to **enforce its security**.

Banks may also seek **guarantees** that the borrower will repay. So, for example, a bank may lend to an **operating company** in a group (a company that carries on part of the group's business) but may seek a guarantee from the **holding company** (the top company) in the group. This is often called a **parent company guarantee** (because the holding company is the parent of all the others in the group, which are its subsidiaries).

An assurance that falls short of a full guarantee is called a **comfort letter** to reassure the bank that, as the borrowing company's principal or sole shareholder, the parent company will keep the borrowing company in funds and not allow it to become insolvent.

A **debenture** is a type of security issued by a public company.

Syndicated Loans

If a company wants to borrow more than one bank is prepared to lend (because the size of the loan will expose the bank to too much of the borrower's risk) the bank may bring in a syndicate (pool) of other banks to lend to the borrower on the same terms.

This is called a **syndicated loan**. There is one loan agreement and all the banks sign it.

Acquisition Finance

One use of syndicated loans is in M&A transactions, where bank lending is called **acquisition finance**.

As you now know, acquisitions are generally funded by the bidder's equity in a share-for-share acquisition. But debt finance is often more attractive to the target's shareholders (they get money not the buyer's shares), the bidder (since the costs are tax-deductible whereas dividends are paid out of after-tax income) and the bidder's shareholders since any additional issue of equity may depress the bidder's share price (since there are more shares in issue).

An acquisition which uses a very high level of debt is often called an **LBO** (**leveraged buy out** where 'leveraged' means **highly geared**, that is, a lot of debt in proportion to equity).

Sometimes a lender may want the option of turning its loan (or part of the loan) into shares if the bought-out business does well, in which case that debt is called **mezzanine finance** (mezzanine is a floor that's mid-way between two others; so this type of debt is mid-way between debt and equity). It is convertible from debt into equity.

Asset Finance

A company can use a loan to fund the plant and equipment it uses in its businesses.

But **asset finance** (also called **finance leasing**) is a tax-efficient way of doing this where the bank will buy the asset and lease it (lend it) to the company for it to use in its business.

It's tax efficient because government provides tax allowances to encourage industry to reinvest in new equipment and so remain competitive.

Because buying a piece of equipment can be a drain on cash flow, companies may buy equipment they feel they need to own (rather than just use) by instalments. Ways of paying by instalments include **hire purchase** and **conditional sale**.

DEBT: BONDS

So far we've been looking at types of loan and loan-based funding. But there is another type of debt called a **bond**.

The word 'bond' has several meanings. Confusingly, one meaning is guarantee (which we've just been looking at) as in 'posting a bond' to guarantee that something happens (a **completion bond** is used to ensure that a construction project doesn't run out of money, for instance).

Tradable Debt Securities

But its more important meaning is a piece of paper that is simply an 'I owe you' or IOU. This is what companies (and governments) issue when they want to raise substantial amounts. Whereas a loan may be provided by just one or a few banks (in a syndicate), a bond will be issued in what are called the **international capital markets** and so may be bought by a much wider array of financial institutions.

This makes the **cost of borrowing** lower (the more lenders there are willing to provide debt to you, the less you will have to pay – basic supply and demand). One reason for this is that it is easier to sell a bond than a loan. This ease of transfer is called tradability – bonds are called **tradable debt securities** (security here doesn't mean charge but means a bond or a share from the days when they were made of card and were security printed so they couldn't be forged – nowadays they are electronic entries). So bonds can be very effective for borrowers that want to raise big amounts of money. Borrowing by issuing a bond is often called **debt issuance** where the borrower is the **issuer**.

Fixed Income Instruments

A company that wants to raise, say, £100 million (bond issues are only worth doing for substantial amounts) will issue an IOU that says: 'I will pay you £100 million pounds in 10 years' time and in the meantime I will pay you interest of 5%.'

Whoever buys the bond will hand over £100 million to the company and in return the bondholder will receive £5 million (which is 5% of £100 million) every year for 10 years and at the end of the 10 years will get the £100 million back again. It's as simple as that, except that instead of one bondholder providing £100 million, there will be lots of different institutional investors buying smaller amounts.

A bond that pays a rate of interest that is fixed (as here) is called a **fixed income bond**. There are bonds that pay a floating rate of interest where the interest rate will move with prevailing interest rates over the life of the bond. These are called **floating rate notes** (note and bond mean the same thing). But most bonds are fixed income instruments.

Basis Points

Because the amounts being borrowed are so large, the interest rate isn't expressed in terms of whole percentages but in hundredths of a per cent, which are called **basis points**. So if a company is borrowing at 1.5% more than the Bank of England base rate (the usual borrowing benchmark in the UK since it's the rate at which the UK government borrows in the financial markets) the company is said to be borrowing at '150 basis points above base'.

High Yield Bonds

Finally there are bonds called **high yield bonds**. These are bonds that are paying a high rate of interest in relation to the amount being borrowed. A bond may go down in value in the market if there are concerns about whether the borrower is able to repay it. So, using the example above, if that £100 million bond went down in value in the market so that investors were only prepared to pay £50 million for it, its yield (interest expressed as a percentage of the market value) will have gone up to 10% because it is still paying £5 million in interest a year and £5 million is 10% of £50 million, hence high yield.

Why am I telling you all this? Not to turn you into a financier, but because money is the lifeblood of business and these are terms that business people are familiar with, so you need to be too.

EQUITY: TYPES OF SHARES

That completes the debt picture. Returning briefly to **equity funding** (investment provided by shareholders), there aren't as many variations.

You can get different types of shares such as **preference shares** (holders of preference shares get dividends before **ordinary shareholders**). You get **warrants**, which entitle holders to buy shares at a certain price. And you get **convertible bonds** which are bonds (debt instruments) that convert into shares. Why do they do this? Because a lender may want to become a shareholder if the business proves to be successful. So instead of making a loan (from which it will get interest and the return of the principal only), it buys a convertible bond.

OTHER FINANCIAL PRODUCTS IMPORTANT TO BUSINESS

Two other financial terms that you need to be aware of are insurance and hedging.

Insurance

You know what **insurance** is: it's paying a **premium** to an insurance company in return for having a risk covered. If you insure your holiday and it gets cancelled you get the cost back. Companies insure too. But often they may decide to bear the risk themselves and this is called **self-insurance**.

Hedging

Hedging is about the use of financial instruments called **derivatives** (because they are derived from other financial instruments or transactions) to protect against risk.

There are three types of derivative: swaps, options and futures (also called forwards).

Swaps

An **interest-rate swap** enables a company that has one type of interest rate (say, fixed) to swap it for another (say, floating) – which it may want to do if it thinks interest rates are going down but it doesn't want to **unwind** the loan completely (because doing so would be more expensive than entering into the swap). A **currency swap** enables a company to swap one currency for another which a multinational operating in many countries may want to do.

Options

An **option** enables a company to fix a price at which to buy or sell something in case that price starts to change. So an airline may take out an option to buy aviation fuel at a specific price if it is worried that the price may have increased by the time it comes to need the fuel.

Forwards Or Futures

Alternatively it may decide to buy the fuel at today's price for delivery in, say, six months' time when it will need it. This is called a **forward** and, if it is an instrument that you can trade on an exchange, it is called a **future**.

CHAPTER 6

MONEY AND BUSINESS (2):

CASH FLOW AND PROFIT

Cash flow – profit – start-up capital – burn rate – insolvent – wound up – bankrupt – factoring – invoice discounting – income – sales – gross revenue – turnover – outgoings – expenditure – net revenue – margin – capital – fixed assets – working capital requirement – book-keeper – accountants – auditors – previous financial year – current financial year – quarterly interim figures – balance sheet – profit & loss (P&L) – creditors – current debtors – current assets – liabilities – fixed costs – overheads – variable costs – goodwill – retained earnings – return on investment (ROI) – net present value – amortisation – depreciation – key performance indicators (KPI) – budget – business plan – forecast – report – quarterly – first quarter – financial year – prospects – future market conditions – gearing – income gearing – pre-tax profit margin – return on capital employed (ROCE) – total business return – cash flow return on investment (CFROI) – free cash flow – discounted cash flow – economic value add (EVA) – cost of capital – economic rent – market value added – total shareholder return – research analyst – indices – market price – price change – price movements – volatile – market capitalisation – gross dividend yield – price/earnings ratio – earnings per share (EPS) – dividend cover – benchmark – proxy

The last chapter was a whistle-stop tour round the different types of funding and financial instruments available to companies. The big message was the difference between debt and equity.

This chapter is about how business uses money and why it needs it. (Surely a business makes money, not consumes it? Well, we'll see.) The big message here is the difference between **cash flow** and **profit** and why, for a young business, cash flow matters more than profit, at least initially.

Understand the difference between debt and equity and between cash flow and profit and you will know the most important fundamentals about business.

Why Cash Flow Matters Before Profit

When a business starts it needs a great deal of money. Let's say I make cakes. I decide to start a business on my kitchen table, making and selling cakes. I need a website to advertise them. I need a logo and a design so I need to commission a graphic artist. I need accounting and tax advice. I need a way of delivering the cakes. I may decide to talk a stall in the local market. And if my business takes off I will need lots of ingredients. Instead of making a couple of cakes a day I may need to make ten or even twenty. At the start I will always be spending more than my cake sales are bringing in as I build up my business and build up customers and sales. I may decide to become a company.

All these things take money.

I will put in my own savings and get family and friends to put in money as well. This will be equity (called **start-up capital**). I and they will have shares. I will borrow from my local bank. This is debt. So far so good.

But the point at the moment is that what I need is cash flow – enough money coming in to keep me going. I hope over time to make a profit but if I don't have enough money to meet all of those expenses mentioned above I won't stay in business long enough to make a profit.

You'll see from what we've just covered that businesses, especially when they've just started, need a lot of money. The speed with which a start-up consumes cash is called the **burn rate**.

Profit Is Not The Only Aim Of Business

When anyone is asked what the purpose of business is, they will tend to say: 'To make a profit.' That is true but doesn't go far enough.

It's a bit like saying a football team's aim is to win a game. Yes, but it wants to do well over the season, please its fans, develop new players and play a role in the local community. Business is just like that. Profit is a way of keeping score. But it is not the only purpose behind business. It also wants to innovate, to please its customers, to give its employees meaningful work and develop them and to be a good corporate citizen to its stakeholders and community.

Further, profit is not the primary aim of business. The primary aim of business is to stay in business. And for that you need cash flow. This is really important and I only realised it when I ran my own business.

Money In The Till

Imagine you are a shopkeeper. At the end of each day you look in the till to see how much money you have there. That's the money you've taken in from customers over the day. Out of that you've paid your suppliers who've been in today, the wholesalers who provide you with goods to stock on the shelves. You may have paid, say, an electricity bill and the driver of your delivery van his weekly wages. The point is: you have had money in the till to do so; and when you open up the shop tomorrow you'll have cash in the till to meet some of tomorrow's outgoings as well.

Profit Is A Quarterly Calculation

Have you made a profit? The truth is: you don't know. You'll find that out at the end of the quarter (businesses divide the year into four quarters, each of three months) when your book-keeper tots up all your income and all your outgoings and you see if one is greater than the other. If income is greater than outgoings, you've made a profit; if not, you've made a loss.

Now, here's the thing. Suppose at the end of each quarter you've made a loss of, say, five pounds. But you have forty pounds in savings. In theory that forty pounds will meet your quarterly losses for eight quarters, which is two years. So, even if you make a loss you have reserves that will keep you going for two years. However, if you don't have any money in your till or you don't have enough to pay off your suppliers, driver, the utility bills and the rent on a day-by-day basis you will go out of business – unless you use that forty pounds and/or borrow from the bank. But the point is that lack of cash flow is an immediate issue whereas lack of profit isn't.

Why Lack Of Cash Flow Kills Start-Ups

Over time all businesses need to make a profit to keep going but they don't always have to make a profit each quarter. But they do always need cash in the till. And when you are starting out as a business and have lots of outgoings as you start to establish yourself and not much money coming in because people aren't aware of you yet, that is when the lack of cash flow can cripple you and doom your business.

Start-ups go out of business because of lack of cash flow not lack of profit. You can be, on paper, a very profitable business where customers are prepared to pay high prices and your outgoings are much smaller. But unless you have those customers coming in and buying and providing you with cash flow, you soon won't have a business at all. As mentioned earlier, a company that runs out of cash will be **insolvent** (companies become insolvent and are **wound up**; individuals become **bankrupt**).

Factoring and Invoice Discounting

One way of helping cash flow is **factoring** (also known as **invoice discounting**). Factoring is where a bank buys a company's receivables for immediate cash: so, let's say, I sell lots of widgets but I don't want to have to wait for my customers to pay or chase up those that don't. What I want is the cash now – for instance, to enhance my cash flow. So I sell those debts to my bank for, say, 90% of their value. I get 90 pence in the pound immediately for no hassle and the bank gets the other 10% for chasing up the debts and, also, as interest on the 90% between the time it pays that money to me and when it gets paid by my customers. A lot of businesses use factoring – it's a specialist area of banking in its own right.

Capital And Income

We've seen how a start-up needs capital (money to start with) and cash flow (money coming in). In accounting terms these are called capital and income. Accounting is how a business keeps score – how it tells how well it is doing.

Income is what a business earns on a day-to-day basis from trading. It's also called **sales** or **gross revenue** or **turnover**. From that it subtracts its **outgoings**, also known as **expenditure**. The difference is its profit. Profit is also called **net revenue**, 'net' meaning after deduction of outgoings. Profit at a micro level is called **margin** – it's the profit you make per unit of production after deducting the cost of the raw materials and manufacturing that go into the finished product.

Capital is the money a business needs in order to be in business, in order to fund its premises, equipment and so on. Capital is what it raises from shareholders (equity) and in long-term debt funding from banks and bondholders. It uses this money to finance its **fixed assets**. These are parts of the business that are there day-in, day-out because they help it manufacture its goods or provide its services.

Working Capital Requirement

Of course a company may also borrow to fund its cash flow (the difference between its day-to-day gross income and outgoings). This funding 'gap' is a business's **working capital requirement**. Although the use of the term 'capital' is confusing here, at least 'working capital' implies that it's to do with income rather than long-term, real 'capital'.

How A Business Looks After The Numbers

A business will have a **book-keeper** to keep track of its daily income and expenditure and will use **accountants** to draw up its detailed accounts. All public companies are required to appoint **auditors**. These are accountants whose job is to tell shareholders how their company has done over the last 12 months (called the **previous financial year** as opposed to the **current financial year**). Public companies generally also provide **quarterly interim figures**. They are called quarterly because they cover the previous three months and they are interim because they provide a less detailed overview pending (or as a stop-gap) till the next annual accounts.

A company's annual accounts comprise two documents. One is the **balance sheet**. The other is the **P&L (profit & loss)** account. They do different things. The balance sheet tells you how much capital is employed in the business, where the capital is from and what it's being used to fund in the business. It's like a snapshot of the company and relates to a single point in time. By contrast the P&L account records the business's income and expenses over a period and tells you whether it's made a profit or a loss – there's an accounting convention that a loss is stated in brackets so a loss of £50,000 would be written as (50,000) or if, as is usual, the figures are stated in thousands, then (50).

The Language Of Numbers

Before going any further it's worth saying that business leaders understand the language of numbers. They can read a balance sheet and a P&L account as if they're reading a newspaper. Numbers paint a picture of how a business is doing. By looking at the capital employed, the fixed assets, the working capital requirement, the cash flow and so on you can tell a lot about the health of a business. But a business is a living, breathing entity whose health changes from day to day. So numbers can never provide a perfect scientific analysis.

Because accountants deal in numbers, they understand the language of business and this makes them more commercially aware than, say, lawyers or surveyors. The rest of us have to work hard to be as commercially aware without having their precise grasp of how numbers work in business.

Why Numbers Aren't Boring

One other thing. This may strike you as dull. If business is just about numbers and money, it's boring isn't it? Wrong. Entrepreneurs and bosses who create businesses and make them massive will in the process make themselves rich (they do this through getting performance bonuses when their company does well and having share options – the chance to buy shares in their company at a low price). Yet they still keep on working.

You hear of multimillionaires who still go to work, of people in their seventies who refuse to retire. Why? It's because business is a huge game to them – it's a way of pitting their wits against their competitors. The money isn't important to them – often very rich business people continue to live in modest houses, drive modest cars and have modest holidays. For them it's about business as sport (which is why a lot of business people are huge sports fans) and the money is just a way of keeping score. It's also why many business people who stop working in order to retire often die soon afterwards. Business is their life. Without it they have nothing to live for.

So what follows may seem boring. But it's the business stories the numbers tell that are interesting.

Balance Sheet

A simple balance sheet tells you:

Where the company's funding comes from:

- Shareholders
- Lenders (bank)
- Money owed to suppliers (**creditors**)

And what it is being used to fund:

- Land and buildings
- Machinery and equipment
- Raw materials
- Finished products
- Money owed by customers (**current debtors**)
- Money at the bank

Debtors And Creditors

Note that creditors are people you owe money to (they are giving you 'credit') and debtors are people who owe money to you (they have debts owing to you). I hope that, looked at like this, it's beginning to make sense.

Land and buildings and machinery and equipment are needed in the business long-term so they are the fixed assets mentioned earlier. The rest are used up and replaced and so are called **current assets**.

So let's set this out as a traditional balance sheet does it:

Capital and liabilities	£'000	Assets		£'000
Issued share capital	15	Fixed assets		
		Land / buildings	9	
		Machinery / equipment	6	
Loan from bank	5	Current assets		
Current liabilities		Raw materials	2	
Creditors	2	Finished products	3	
		Current debtors	1	
		Cash	1	
	22			22

You will see that the left hand side (capital and liabilities – **liabilities** means what the company owes) and the right hand side (assets) both add up to the same figure. In other words, they 'balance'. If they didn't, it wouldn't be a balance sheet. And just to make it absolutely complete we would need to give it a title specifying the date on which it is accurate (businesses are always dynamic and changing so the balance sheet relates to one specific date) such as: *Balance sheet of ABC Ltd as at 31 December 2012.*

P&L

Now let's turn to the profit and loss account. Here you total up your expenses and your income to see whether you have made a profit or loss:

Expenditure

- Rent
- Rates
- Interest paid to the bank for the loan
- Salaries
- Raw materials
- Electricity
- Phone bill

Then you add up your revenue from sales to give you your income, and set this out, like the balance sheet, so one is opposite the other. Some costs are **fixed costs** – the business has them however busy it is and they tend to be long-term (often called **overheads**); whereas others vary in line with how busy the business is and are **variable costs**, hence what follows:

Expenditure	'000	Income	£'000
Fixed costs		Revenue from sales	??
Rates	1		
Salaries	8		
Interest paid to bank	2		
Variable costs			
Raw materials	15		
Electricity	2		
Phone bill	1		
	29		??

You'll see that it isn't complete. We know the outgoings for the period were £29,000. If the revenue was more than that, we have made a profit; if less, a loss.

A profit….

Expenditure	£'000	Income	£'000
Fixed costs		Revenue from sales	32
Rates	1		
Salaries	8		
Interest paid to bank	2		
Variable costs			
Raw materials	15		
Electricity	2		
Phone bill	1		
Net profit	*3*		
	32		32

.... or a loss

Expenditure	£'000	Income	£'000
Fixed costs		Revenue from sales	26
Rates	1		
Salaries	8		
Interest paid to bank	2		
Variable costs			
Raw materials	15		
Electricity	2		
Phone bill	1		
		Net loss	*3*
	29		29

We put the profit or loss figure on the side it needs to go to make the two columns add up.

And just for completeness we need to specify the period to which it relates: *Profit & loss account for ABC Ltd 1 January - 31 December 2012.*

You may come across two things that I haven't mentioned here. One is a balance sheet item, the other is a P&L entry.

Goodwill As A Balance Sheet Item

The first is **goodwill**. This is often included in balance sheets on the right hand side as a fixed asset and generally means that bit of a business which represents why customers come to it (its reputation) that isn't just a matter of its fixed assets.

It is often used where a company is taken over and what is paid for it is more than its actual assets are worth. The excess represents goodwill – that is, the worth of the company over and above the assets it owns. Goodwill appears under the 'fixed assets' heading and is used to make the company's capital side and assets side balance.

Note also, while we're on balance sheets, that if any previous profits aren't paid out to shareholders by way of dividend they are called **retained earnings** and become part of a company's capital and liabilities.

Depreciation As A P&L Entry

The other, the P&L item, is depreciation. This is a figure that accountants put in to allow for the 'wear and tear' that the assets in a business incur as they are being used, which means that in due course they will need to be replaced. So each year the company allows a bit for depreciation to reflect the fact that sooner or later the equipment will wear out and money will need to be spent replacing it. This is an expense of the business so it appears on the left hand side and reduces the profit or increases the loss:

Profit & loss account for ABC Ltd 1 January - 31 December 2012

Expenditure	£'000	Income	£'000
Fixed costs		Revenue from sales	32
Rates	1		
Salaries	8		
Interest paid to bank	2		
Depreciation allowance	*1*		
Variable costs			
Raw materials	15		
Electricity	2		
Phone bill	1		
Net profit	2		
	32		32

Accountants use a variety of terms in connection with businesses. Some in the following list we've already encountered:

- **Return on investment (ROI)** is the amount of income that is expected to be generated by investing a given amount of capital in a project.
- **Net present value** – the value of a future return discounted (i.e. reduced by the interest implicit between now and then) to give a current value.
- **Amortisation** – the reduction in debt by repaying it in instalments.
- **Depreciation** – the reduction in the value of an asset in the business to reflect the wear and tear it suffers and to allow for the cost of its replacement.

- **Key performance indicators** (**KPI**) – the principal financial measures which tell a business whether it is on target.

- **Budget** – a plan setting out how much can be spent in the business over a given period.

- **Business plan** – often underpins a strategy, setting out future income and expenditure as well as items such as level of staffing, size of premises, etc.

- **Forecast** – prediction of future sales / turnover.

- **Report** – financial review of a period just ended.

- **Quarterly** – every three months.

- **First quarter** – first three months of the financial year (often written as Q1, with the others as Q2, Q3, Q4).

- **Financial year** – the 12-month period at the end of which the business draws up its annual report; can be the same as the calendar year (January-December) or the tax year (April-March) but doesn't have to be either.

- **Balance sheet** – periodic snapshot of the capital (equity and debt) employed in the business and the assets that capital is funding.

- **Profit & Loss** – statement of income and expenditure over a period showing whether or not a profit or loss is generated.

When shareholders receive their company's annual report it contains two types of information:

- Words, providing details of the management's background together with their views of the company's **prospects** and **future market conditions**; and

- Figures, providing financial data.

The financial data will include:

- **Gearing** – the ratio of shareholders' funds (equity) to liabilities (debt); you can now see that gearing is about how much borrowing a company has in proportion to its equity – I mentioned earlier that companies often like to be highly geared because it is tax efficient but also because it enables them to expand more quickly than their competitors (provided they're doing the right things in terms of products, customers and strategy). A company that gets this wrong can become too highly geared to pay the interest and then runs the risk of becoming insolvent. So a high level of gearing can be risky because borrowings are high relative to equity, but it may also indicate that the business is expanding fast by maximising the capital available to it.

- **Income gearing** – the ratio of interest payable on the company's debt to the profits out of which that interest is paid (this is similar to the role of dividend cover in relation to the company's equity base); again, the higher the ratio the more the company may be stretched to service its debt if profits fall, but it may also be a positive indication of a company straining at the leash to expand as fast as possible.

- **Pre-tax profit margin** – this measures the profits earned per pound sterling of sales. Profit margin indicates how efficient a company is, how sustainable its competitive advantage is and how resilient it is likely to be if faced with adverse market conditions.

- **Return on capital employed (ROCE)** – this is a key performance measure of what economists call economic rent (see below) and is indicative of a company's efficiency in using its assets funded by its capital, and its ability to generate earnings that will provide future dividends and avoid future cash flow problems.

Internal Ways Of Assessing ROCE

Since a principal financial role of a company is to create value for its shareholders, the managers of the business use a variety of ways to measure the return on the shareholders' funds, including:

- **Total business return** – which captures changes in the value of a business over a period and the cash flows generated by it during that period.

- **CFROI (cash flow return on investment)** – which compares the cumulative cash invested in a business with the cash the business is producing, while allowing for the ageing of assets employed in the business as well as inflation.

- **Free cash flow** – operating cash less interest on loans, taxes and investment.

- **Discounted cash flow** – which is used to evaluate possible projects by assessing how much the capital required to fund the project would generate if invested elsewhere, and then comparing that return to the project's expected return: if that return is less than the alternative, the project should not be undertaken (the reference to 'discounted' is because the future return has to be turned into today's money by subtracting the intervening return to get back to 'net present value' – but the key question is what discount to apply).

- **EVA (economic value added)** – a measure invented by consultants Stern Stewart which seeks to calculate the value of a business activity that is left over after subtracting the cost of executing that activity and the opportunity cost (i.e. what could have been generated by an alternative activity).

ROCE, however it is measured, connects with strategy. I said earlier that the point of strategy is to create sustainable competitive advantage. To couch this in economic terms, a company is expected to generate returns that are consistently greater than its **cost of capital** (the money invested in it). It is these returns that are called **economic rent** by economists who say that a sustainable competitive advantage leads to above-normal rent. Of course, such rents will attract new entrants who drive down economic rents – which takes us back to Porter's Five Forces.

For their part, shareholders consider:

- **Market value added** which is the difference between the current market value of a company (i.e. its stock market value) and the capital contributed by shareholders. If it is positive, then the company has added value; if not, it has destroyed shareholder value.

- **Total shareholder return** which measures three cash flows associated with a share: purchase price (cash out); dividend stream (cash in) and value realised on sale (cash in).

The point of all of these measures is that different ones are appropriate at different times and for different purposes. Different companies (and indeed different industries) present their accounts in different ways and use different conventions and financial ratios. International accounting standards differ markedly, not just in terminology and presentation, but in the treatment of many activities such as mergers, pensions, reserves, finance leases and the value of financial instruments. These differences result from different philosophies (such as the purpose of accounts: to inform shareholders or to protect creditors?) and different general principles underlying accounting standards in different countries.

So all these measures have their limitations. Unless you are an accountant or a management consultant, you don't need to understand these measures fully. You just need to recognise what business people are talking about when they mention them.

Investment Analysis

Now, let's broaden the picture out again. You may not be a shareholder in a company but you are interested in business and want to read how different businesses are doing. If you are a **research analyst** you will plough through stacks of companies' annual reports (which are public documents so anyone can see them). But if you just want a snapshot you will look at a real-time financial news service like Reuters or Bloomberg or read the *Financial Times* (the newspaper printed on pink paper).

The *Financial Times* runs a number of **indices** in conjunction with the London Stock Exchange (including the FTSE 100 mentioned earlier). Typically, you will come across some or all of the following information about a company's shares:

- **Market price** – its value at the market close the previous day (usually an average of all the quotes provided by the various market makers).

- **Price change** – yesterday's closing price compared to the day before.

- **Price movements** – the highest and lowest prices over the previous 12 months: this shows you how **volatile** (up and down) a company's share price is.

- **Market capitalisation** – how much the company is worth (arrived at by multiplying the number of shares in issue by the share price): this tells you how big the company is.

- **Gross dividend yield** – the dividend divided by the share price expressed as a percentage: this tells you how much income return you are getting for your capital investment in the company's shares. Investors wanting income (dividends) will go for a high yield.

- **Price/earnings ratio** – the p/e ratio is the share price divided by the **earnings per share** (**EPS**) with EPS being the net profit over its most recent trading year divided by the number of shares in issue. The p/e ratio is used as a measure to compare how much dividend you get for the price of the share between companies in the same sector (p/e ratios differ between sectors). Another way of looking at it is that the resulting figure tells you how many years it will take on the basis of the current dividend stream to get back the cost of the share. The p/e ratio is the single most commonly used way of assessing company performance. Investors looking for growth (increase in share value over time) will look for high price/earnings.

- **Dividend cover** – the ratio of profits to dividends: the extent to which the current dividend is 'covered' by current profit: the better the cover the more cautious the company is being in not paying out all of its profits to shareholders but retaining earnings to fund expansion.

When they say on the news that the FTSE 100 rose or fell by a certain number of points, that is an average figure taken across the entire FTSE 100. So the FTSE 100 is a **benchmark** or **proxy** for how the UK financial markets are doing.

Mention of financial markets makes this a good moment to broaden the picture out even further and to set business in the context of government and macro-economics, as we'll see in the next chapter.

CHAPTER 7

BUSINESS, GOVERNMENT AND MACRO-ECONOMICS

Private sector – public sector – charities – non-governmental organisations (NGOs) – third sector – communist economies – capitalist economies – privatisation – global initial public offering – commercialisation – franchise – concession – trade sale – market liberalisation – public private partnership (PPP) – private finance initiative (PFI) – off balance sheet (OBS) – restructured – reorganisation – trading arrangements – nationalisation – monopolies – cartels – competition authorities – regulation – public sector borrowing requirement – gross domestic product (GDP) – balance of payments – supply – demand – inflation – retail price index (RPI) – unemployment – geopolitics – macro-economics

I started this book by saying that everything provided commercially is because we want it. It is the job of business to serve our needs, either directly through B2C or indirectly through B2B.

The Private, Public and Third Sectors

Of course, not all our needs are provided by business, by the **private sector** as it is called. Some of our needs are provided by the state, also known as government or the **public sector** (public because it is owned by us, by society). There is also an intermediate sector made up of **charities** and **NGOs (non-governmental organisations)** which aren't commercial companies either. This is called the voluntary sector (because it depends in large part on unpaid workers volunteering their time) or the **third sector**.

Some things we get (and expect to get) from the state: defence provided by the armed forces; protection in society by the police; a fire service to stop our homes from burning down; roads and pavements. We pay for these with taxes. Some things we expect to get from business: food and clothing, for instance, which we go out and buy. Some things may be provided by either or both: education; healthcare; transport.

Capitalism And Communism

In fact the boundary between the public and private sectors is fuzzy and subject to constant change. In **communist economies** the idea is that the state owns everything including (as Karl Marx put it) the means of production and provides everything we need. There is no profit motive as such and no competition: there's no need for either. In **capitalist economies** capital (money) is channelled to those businesses that can put it to best use. Their reward is profit which they use to re-invest in the business to expand it and to reward their investors.

Which is better? That's a question for politicians and political scientists. My view is that countries need different systems at different stages of their development. A very poor country dependent on an agrarian (agricultural) economy with very little by way of infrastructure (roads, schools, hospitals) may be better off as a communist state so that everyone gets a bit of everything (food, clothing, healthcare, education). A developed economy is better off with capitalism which encourages innovation and change. But that's just my view.

We live at a time in the world when most countries are either capitalist or are moving towards it. This is why the boundaries between public and private sectors are porous. Over the last fifty years there has been a trend for communist states to begin to embrace capitalism and for capitalist countries to move even more business from the public to the private sectors.

Privatisation

In fact whole industries can move between the two. **Privatisation** is where an entire state-owned industry, often a monopoly, is moved into the private sector by turning it into a business with owners and customers. Privatisation has been used in virtually all sectors, from energy production and transmission (oil, gas and electricity, for example), utilities (such as water), transport (ranging from airlines and airports to roads, bridges and ports) to mineral and other resource extraction, industrial plant projects, waste treatment processes and financial services.

By attracting private sector investment, these old state enterprises can modernise more quickly and improve the services they offer consumers, often in newly-opened up competitive markets which offer lower prices.

Commercialisation

There are different types of privatisation. At its purest and grandest, it is about selling off state-owned industries often in their entirety, for instance through a **global initial public offering** where shares in the industry are offered around the world to investors. But less extreme versions include **commercialisation** (subjecting an activity to private sector competition, which may include joint ventures between the state and the private sector), the grant of a **franchise** or **concession** (allowing the private sector to offer that service) or a **trade sale** (selling the industry to a private-sector entity already in that business). All of these cases may be accompanied by **market liberalisation** (removing state monopolies so anyone can compete).

PPP And PFI

Often government will privatise something because government lacks the funds to develop it or improve it or just to raise money to meet government expenditure. Sometimes government will look to private sector involvement or financing in big infrastructure projects (like roads, railways, hospitals, power stations) which government alone cannot fund.

This can be undertaken through **public private partnership** (**PPP**) or **private finance initiative** (**PFI**) transactions. For example, a private contractor may build a road and be allowed by government to charge users a toll (a fee) for using it. Out of this the contractor recovers the cost of building the road plus a profit but with the agreement that after, say, 30 years, the road reverts to public ownership and the government takes it over.

Off Balance Sheet

Aside from the political desire to look prudent by postponing the real cost to a time when it is no longer in power, the only real advantage to government of doing this is that it is able to bring many more projects on-stream than by finding the money to build them one at a time. Privatisation enables the state to keep the capital cost of modernisation **OBS (off balance sheet)**, which makes it look financially prudent.

Restructuring Prior To Privatisation

All privatisations have at least one aspect in common: the need to attract willing buyers or investors. The buyer (whether a business or investors) will want to know what they are buying. This usually means that the industry in question has to be **restructured** to make it attractive.

This may be done through a **reorganisation**, to separate the industrial activity from the rest of government, and so identify the revenue stream and cost basis attributable to it.

Trading arrangements – often with other public sector entities – are formalised, ownership of particular assets is established and state guarantees are removed. The enterprise is turned into one or more companies whose shares are owned by the government. Privatisation then consists of selling those shares to the private sector.

Nationalisation

The opposite of privatisation is when industry moves from private to public ownership. This is called **nationalisation**. Some industries – such as defence – are usually regarded as so critical to national security that they will always remain in public ownership, meaning that the government owns them. In some countries this extends to arms manufacture, electricity generation and so on.

Sometimes nationalisation is the result of a financial crisis: many banks were nationalised in the global financial crisis because they would otherwise have gone bust. Note here that the term reorganisation or restructuring is also used when a business goes bust – technically, the term is 'becomes insolvent' – and has to be rescued.

Competition And Regulation

Many state-owned industries are **monopolies** (there is only one provider). Economists don't like monopolies because the lack of competition can lead to inefficiency, poor innovation and high prices to consumers.

So the state becomes involved with the private sector in another way – through competition and regulation.

The state passes and enforces laws that encourage competition in order to avoid monopolies and **cartels** (a cartel is a group of companies working together to fix prices). These are anti-competitive and bad for consumers. Some countries (and the European Union) have government agencies called **competition authorities** that enforce laws preventing businesses from becoming market dominant or gaining monopoly advantage for this reason.

Competition law is a form of **regulation** designed to protect the consumer. But the state regulates business in other ways, for instance in preventing pharmaceuticals from being sold without proper testing and licensing, or ensuring that foodstuffs are properly labelled with their ingredients and are date-stamped.

The state also encourages business by providing tax incentives (mentioned earlier in the context of asset finance). It may provide regional grants to encourage businesses to open factories in areas of economic deprivation to boost employment.

So the relationship between business and government is symbiotic (inter-dependent).

Running The Public And Third Sectors Like Businesses

There is another way in which the public and private sectors interact, and that is that the public sector is itself becoming more business-minded. Government has only two sources of income to run the country: taxes and borrowing. If a government taxes its citizenry too highly it will be voted out of office. Whatever it borrows has to be repaid (known as the **public sector borrowing requirement**). So government has become more commercial in its outlook.

This is why, even if you want to be a teacher or a health worker or work in the police service, you will need to be commercially aware, in order to do more with less resource.

The same is true of the third sector. Charities are funded by public donations. The people leading them have to be commercially aware in order to make the most of those donations. The third sector is run along business lines too.

So, doctors working in the national health service need commercial awareness to run their practices, even though they are funded by government. Charities, raising money from the public and then spending it to fund good causes, need to be commercially aware if their outgoings are not to exceed their income.

Business, Government And Macro-Economics

Companies make up a country's private sector which is the principal contributor to a country's economic prosperity.

Government looks closely at the country's **GDP** (**gross domestic product**) which measures annual output in goods and services. This is broken down into private and government consumption, investment and exports (known as the **balance of payments** – if they are positive it means the country is exporting more than it's importing; if not, the country is consuming more than it is producing).

Government studies output by industrial sector using a range of measures from manufacturing output and retail sales to housing starts (new house-building projects begun).

Supply And Demand

A key economic principle here is supply and demand.

Supply is the quantity that producers are willing to sell at a given price.

Demand is the quantity that consumers have the capacity and willingness to buy at a given price.

When the price is lower, demand will increase; when the price is higher, producers will make more so supply will increase. The intersection is the equilibrium point when the market 'clears' (supply and demand match).

Inflation

Supply and demand drive **inflation** (the erosion of the real value of money). A little inflation is all right (it tends to push house prices steadily up so people feel richer). But a lot is bad because it discourages people from saving and hits those on low incomes like the poor and pensioners. So government monitors inflation through a variety of measures – including the **retail price index** (**RPI**) which is based on a 'basket' of typical household spending.

Unemployment

Supply and demand also affect **unemployment**. In the long run economic performance can be enhanced only by increasing employment and, therefore, output. Supply-side economics is the use of incentives (such as lower tax) to increase the level of full employment.

Government is itself a key component of the economy, as an employer (the NHS is the biggest single employer in Europe) and consumer (consumption taking the form of expenditure on everything from military equipment to schools).

Government has to pay for unemployment by providing benefit for those not in work so it is keen to see full employment, which increases the pool of people paying tax, while unemployment has social and political implications (such as increased crime and voter disaffection: an unemployed electorate is unlikely to vote a government back in).

Macro-Economics

Government, business and finance intersect at an international level through **geopolitics** and **macro-economics**.

Each country's economy is unique. They expand and contract at different rates. Some countries are more capitalist than others. So the world economy is a reflection of all of these differences.

But the biggest economies in the world – the US, China, Japan and Germany – have an enormous impact on all the rest. The cliché is that 'if the US sneezes the rest of the world catches cold'. These countries are the biggest exporters. There are other countries such as Brazil and India which are regarded as markets to watch for the future.

The international capital markets (which provide debt and equity funding) push money to where investment is best rewarded. So countries with poor economies or weak government will attract less investment. They will have weak currencies that will not buy them much elsewhere.

Multinational companies will study these factors when deciding where to expand to. They are looking for overseas markets to sell into and countries with cheap natural resources and labour in which to locate their factories.

Geopolitics

Possibly the single biggest geopolitical factor at work internationally is the industrialised world's need for energy, principally oil and gas, and raw materials (for instance for steel).

Oil is running out. The world's peak oil production (when half of the world's available source has been produced) is expected to be reached any year now. Some argue that it's the US's need for oil that drives its foreign policy in the Middle East and beyond.

China, for its part, needed to fuel its recent economic boom through cheap energy and raw materials. It has looked to South America (mainly Venezuela) for oil and Africa for mineral resources. Its political influence is present in both.

CHAPTER 8

WHAT A BUSINESS LOOKS LIKE INSIDE

Chief executive officer (CEO) – board of directors – chairman – executive director – non-executive director – finance director (FD) – chief financial officer (CFO) – chief information officer (CIO) – chief operating officer (COO) – accounts – accounts payable – accounts receivable – administration – back office – business development – buyer – company secretarial – compliance – credit control – estates management – facilities management – finance – fleet – front of house – health & safety (H&S) – human resources (HR) – information technology (IT) – investor relations – intellectual property (IP) – know-how – learning & development (L&D) – legal – library & information – logistics – marketing – middle office – pension fund trustees – petty cash – planning – post room – press relations (PR) – premises – procurement – production – public affairs – public policy – research – research & development (R&D) – risk management – sales – supply chain management – systems – tax – training – treasury – matrix management – organisational design – core – non-core – outsourcing – offshoring – business process re-engineering (BPR) – enterprise resource planning (ERP) – best practice – best-in-class – just-in-time production – continuous improvement (kaizen) – quality movement – Six Sigma – corporate governance – executive pay – remuneration committees – share options – golden hello – golden parachute

From the macro (big) to the micro (small): so far we have looked at how a business serves customers, how it competes and innovates, what strategy is and why it's important, why a company needs money, how it makes money and how all of that financial activity is measured and reported to shareholders and the market.

Now we are going to take a look inside a company to see what people actually do in it. Then we are going to look at what this means for you as you try to become one of those people – an employee, someone working for an organisation (or even running your own business).

From Things To People

So if everything leading up to here has been about things, this is where people become involved.

Of course, I made the point at the beginning that the only reason there are businesses (and governments) at all is to meet the needs of people: you and me as consumers. Now we need to look at you and me as workers, working to earn the money that enables us to be consumers and to buy what we want.

How A Business Is Organised

Take a manufacturing business. You need a factory (production department) where the products are made. You need a marketing department through which they are sold. You need a research and development (R&D) function where improvements to current models are invented and tested. You need a finance department through which income and outgoings go. You can see that all of these are needed to engage with customers.

But there are other, internally focused functions a business also needs. For instance, all large businesses need employees. So you need an HR (human resources) function to deal with hiring people, paying them, dealing with holiday and illness, addressing pension issues and, where necessary, firing them.

You need a department that deals with the premises, managing the property the business occupies, keeping the offices clean, making sure the post gets round to the right people, and so on. The department in charge of this is called facilities or administration.

All businesses use technology so there will also be a technology department. The generic term for many of these functions is back office because they are not directly customer-facing.

Business Leaders

Given all of this, you need someone in charge. At the top of the tree you find the **chief executive officer** (**CEO**) who is charged with day-to-day responsibility for everything in the company.

The company will also have a **board of directors**, of whom the CEO (often called Managing Director) is the most important. The board runs the company and is the executive (it executes the company's plans).

There may also be a **chairman** of the board who is senior to the CEO or MD. The chairman may be an executive chairman but is often non-executive (part-time). The chairman tends to have an outward-facing, strategic and ambassadorial role. But it is the chairman who tends to be instrumental in getting rid of the CEO or MD if the latter isn't doing the job well. An **executive director** is employed in the business day-to-day. A **non-executive director** is part-time and is there in an advisory capacity.

The board of directors will consist of people representing the most important parts of the business. So there will be a **finance director** (**FD**) sometimes called a **chief financial officer** (**CFO**), a commercial director (in charge of marketing), a production director and so on. Although HR may seem a bit back office, people issues are so important that there is usually an HR director on the board.

Others include risk management (which may include legal, compliance and regulatory) to ensure the business is not going to be sunk by an unexpected exposure (legal may be represented separately).

In a manufacturing company, production may be represented along with R&D (research and development). In a know-how business, there may be a **chief information officer** (**CIO**). In an advertising agency, a creative director, and so on. It depends on the particular industry.

There may also be an IT director if systems are 'mission critical'. There may be a director of administration looking after premises and so on.

Increasingly companies have a **chief operating officer** (**COO**) – a term which like CEO, CFO and CIO has come over from the US – who ensures the company is functioning smoothly and who is responsible for admin, systems, HR and some day-to-day financial management.

In fact the bigger a business becomes, the greater the proliferation of specialist roles and functions within it.

Examples of functions you may encounter further down the organisation are set out on the next page in alphabetical order.

Organisational Functions

Accounts
Old name for the Finance function

Accounts Payable
Part of Finance – responsible for paying suppliers

Accounts Receivable
Part of Finance – receives money from customers

Administration
Elastic term that covers everything from the post room and towels in the washrooms to in-house catering, premises and systems

Back Office
New name for Administration – in a bank it often means the settlement function (settling trades)

Business Development
Same as Marketing

Buyer
Deals with suppliers

Company Secretarial
Deals with the submission of forms to ensure the company is properly registered under company law plus the proper convening of shareholders' meetings – in a large group may look after 300-400 companies

Compliance
Deals with regulatory issues – where an industry is closely controlled by law, this function ensures the company is abiding by the law (found in banks)

Credit Control
Chases customers who haven't paid their bills (debtors)

Estates Management
Responsible for the maintenance and legal aspects of the buildings and land the company occupies or owns

Facilities Management
New term for premises, print, mailroom and catering administration

*[handwritten margin notes: law firms / Banks Court BD; * Up Bank inhouse counsel; * ; (Admin)]*

Finance	Responsible for all aspects of money – paying suppliers, getting paid by customers, working capital management and long-term funding of the business
Fleet	Responsible for any vehicles the company has or uses
Front Of House	Those parts of the business that interface with clients in person such as reception and catering in meeting rooms
H&S	Health & Safety – ensuring the company is compliant with applicable laws for the well-being of staff; often part of HR
HR	Human Resources – modern term for 'Personnel' – includes payroll, holidays, sickness records, recruitment, appraisal, performance, disciplinary issues and dismissal; responsible for staff handbooks and policies
Information Technology (IT)	Computer hardware and software, networks, switchboards, phones and devices
Investor Relations	Dealing with shareholders, where the business is a public company
IP	Intellectual property – protects the company's copyrights, patents, brands
Know-How	The company's 'soft' knowledge such as precedents, processes, previous projects
Learning & Development	New term for Training – responsible for staff development, training courses
Legal	Responsible for all legal issues affecting the company, including contracts with suppliers, customers and employees and dealing with any claims brought by or against the company
Library & Information	Old term for Know-How including published sources of external information

Logistics	Also known as supply chain management – responsible for getting the company's products to customers as quickly and cheaply as possible
Marketing	Responsible for the company's image and brand, identifying new markets for products and services
Middle Office	Found in banks and includes legal, compliance, regulatory and risk management – not client-facing (front) and not purely admin (back) but necessary for the organisation's well-being
Pension Fund Trustees	A separate body, often made up of the Finance Director and employees, which looks after the company's pension fund. Because pension funds are subject to increasingly complex regulations, the trustees (who are individuals drawn from the company's employees and management) often turn to professional external trustees to sit alongside them
Petty Cash	Part of Finance, dealing with the float of real money kept at the company
Planning	Often part of Finance, plans the company's future needs for premises, people, funding and so on
Post Room	In charge of internal and external mail. Also known as the mail room. In a multinational can be responsible for complex internal logistics
PR	Press relations – responsible for communications with the world at large (as opposed to communication with customers which is done by Marketing). May report to Marketing
Premises	Old term for Estates Management
Procurement	Same as Buyer but focuses on the process of selecting suppliers and the contracts negotiated with them – works closely with Legal

Production	In manufacturing companies, responsible for the company's output (factories and production lines)
Public Affairs	Sometimes part of PR or Marketing, this deals with government relations – for instance, lobbying against changes in the law and dealing with any trade associations that represent the company's interests
Public Policy	Same as Public Affairs
Research	Often part of Marketing or Library & Information – carries out research into subjects of use to the company, e.g. markets, buying patterns
R&D	Research & Development – in manufacturing companies, in charge of creating new products
Risk Management	Identifies and mitigates risks that the business is exposed to – often includes Legal
Sales	Can be part of Marketing or a separate, related function – this is about making actual sales to customers and includes account management
Supply Chain Management	Same as Logistics
Systems	Same as Information Technology
Tax	Deals with the company's tax position – can be a large department in big companies; often part of Finance or Legal
Training	Old term for Learning & Development
Treasury	Part of Finance, raises short- and long-term funding for the company, invests any surplus cash and deals in the currency market, converting overseas income into pounds

Further complexity is added if a business is spread across a group of companies. Add in regional diversity with a business operating through different companies in different countries and you end up with **matrix management** where no one has a single boss and people have dotted-line reports (having to keep others informed of what they are doing without reporting directly to them).

Periodically businesses become so complex that the organogram (pictorial map of an organisation's internal structure) becomes a mess. At that point they may rethink how they should be organised.

This is a management discipline called **organisational design**. This may lead to restructuring which usually means making people redundant (often in response to cost pressures).

Core And Non-Core

In fact all businesses regularly re-evaluate what is **core** (crucial) and what is **non-core** to their business. They may decide that non-core parts of their business can be subcontracted to an external supplier – a business that specialises in, say, providing HR support to other businesses. This is called **outsourcing**. Relocating (some of) your functions to another, cheaper country is called **offshoring**.

Business Process Re-Engineering

Rethinking how things are done in your business is called **business process re-engineering (BPR)** and may be accompanied by importing integrated technology packages (called **enterprise resource planning** or **ERP**) that integrate all of your back office functions.

All businesses have basic administrative functions, such as having an inventory of their assets. The idea behind ERP is that you can buy a software suite that will do all of this for you in a way that reflects **best practice** across industry (often called **best-in-class**).

Just-In-Time And Continuous Improvement

This quest for business efficiency (a business can only improve profitability by selling more goods at a higher margin or reducing costs or both) has led to waves of production innovation in the last half-century including **just-in-time production** and **continuous improvement** (also known as **kaizen**), both of which were developed in Japan.

With just-in-time production you don't hold big inventories of stock – instead you have only what you need immediately to hand. All businesses now do this.

Continuous improvement means that you never stand still but constantly question how and why you do things. Again, all companies are committed to this these days.

Both are examples of the **quality movement** in industry which is about driving out faulty manufacturing through statistical analysis so that almost no defective products are ever made. The modern form is called **Six Sigma** – a productivity-enhancement programme.

Professional Advisers

A business may call upon management consultants (mentioned previously) to help it do all of this. They are not the only professional advisers (also called professional service firms) that businesses regularly use. Others include law firms, accountancy firms, PR and marketing consultancies, advertising agencies, technology consultants, chartered surveyors (land and premises) and actuaries (pensions).

Corporate Governance

Whoever a business calls upon for help, it's the people at the top who provide leadership to the organisation. Public companies are required to make their management transparent through adherence to voluntary **corporate governance** codes which set out how they should be run and the role of non-executive directors and chairmen to check up on what the directors are doing and how much they are being paid.

Executive pay has been controversial in recent years and **remuneration committees** of public companies are required to ensure that their CEOs, labelled captains of industry by the press, have their remuneration package (pay) pegged to the financial performance of their company (performance-related pay). Often this will be through **share options** (the grant of rights to buy shares in the company). A **golden hello** is a lump sum for joining a company. A **golden parachute** is compensation for being sacked, for instance if the company is taken over.

CHAPTER 9

WORKING INSIDE A BUSINESS

Line manager – function – role – responsibility – debrief – feedback – appraisal – promotion – 360-degree appraisals – resource – business case – delegation – developmental tool – BOOST – training – mentoring – coaching – role play – forum theatre – facilitation – break-out groups – brainstorm – plenary – retreats – off-sites – Alfie Kohn – psychological contract – skill set – lifelong learning – time management – business writing – communication skills – presentation skills – team working – personality types – portfolio workers

An organisation has only one CEO and only a few directors. Very few of us reach those heights. So what do the rest of the employees in an organisation do? Everyone in the world of work has a boss (known as their **line manager**) to whom they report. Everyone works for a **function** (team or department).

On Board

Imagine a cruise ship. The captain is in charge. He's thinking of the ship's direction, how long to get to port and the upcoming weather. Above all he's concerned about the passengers and whether they're having a good time. He has below him various functional heads who make sure the ship goes: the chief engineer who's in charge of making the ship move; the chief navigator who's in charge of the direction it goes in; the chief entertainments officer who's in charge of making sure the passengers are happy; the chief welfare officer who's in charge of making sure everyone on board is safe and well; and so on.

Roles And Responsibilities

The captain walks around the ship making sure everything is in order. If the passengers complain about the food the captain tells the chief welfare officer who has below him someone in charge of catering who has below him the galley staff. So the message goes down to them to make better food. If the weather ahead looks bad the captain has words with the chief navigation officer who sends an order down to whoever is in charge of the charts that they need to plot a different course. And so on. So everyone has a **role** and a **responsibility**. If they didn't there wouldn't be any reason to have them on board taking up valuable space and consuming scarce food.

So it is in business. Everyone has a job, from the CEO down to the person cleaning the floors.

Delegation, Team Work And Feedback

At each rung of command, a job is delegated. So the chief welfare officer delegates to the ship's nurse the job of dealing with passengers and crew who feel sick. The chief welfare officer may have been a doctor himself, so if there's an outbreak of illness the nurse may ask him for guidance or the chief welfare officer may even come into the ship's surgery and work alongside the nurse, even supervising her. This is how people work together as a team in a business.

After the outbreak is over the chief welfare officer and the nurse may hold a **debrief** to see what they can learn for the future – maybe they need more medical supplies of a certain kind on board if they think they will have more outbreaks like this. The chief welfare officer may give the nurse **feedback** on how she did – what she did well, what she could do differently next time.

Appraisal

Every six months or a year the chief welfare officer may carry out a detailed **appraisal** of the nurse's performance with her (this is a more formal version of feedback). They may discuss new skills or expertise the nurse may want to develop or acquire. She may ask for training to get them. She may also ask about her chances of **promotion** once she gets those skills – maybe a transfer to a bigger ship within the cruise line. The chief welfare officer may himself be appraised by the captain.

This way of working ensures that each subordinate undertakes his or her role in the way their superior (line manager) wants, in order to help their line manager achieve the objectives he or she has been set in turn by his or her line manager. Some organisations have **360-degree appraisals** which take into account the views of your subordinates, your colleagues (peers) and clients as well as just your superiors.

Additional Resource

You can see that the chief welfare officer is the nurse's manager. The nurse reports directly to him. If the ship is likely to voyage further through tropical waters and be exposed to more outbreaks the nurse may suggest they need additional **resource** (resource is people and/or money) in the form of additional nurses on board. The chief welfare officer may make this request to the captain who will need to ask the cruise line since additional resource will reduce the profit the ship generates. This will require a strong **business case**.

A Model For Delegation

Sooner or later almost everyone becomes a manager. It's the way you move up an organisation. You may be given training in how to manage others.

For instance, I mentioned **delegation** – getting a subordinate to do a task in the way that you want. Here is, typically, what a manager would do if she were delegating a task to a member of her team.

- She should select an appropriate task for the right developmental reasons (not just to shift something off her desk but because it will help in the team member's development).
- She should then prepare the briefing.
- In the briefing itself, she should:
  - Identify the nature of the task.
  - Check his experience and availability.
  - Specify the output she wants as well as any constraints (such as how much time to spend on it) and the deadline.

- Check his understanding by getting him to reiterate what she has said.
- Check what his first few steps will be.
- Set up an interim monitoring procedure (specifying a midpoint when he can go back and report on progress) to make sure he stays on the right track.

- Once he has done the task, she should provide feedback.
- Finally, she should find further opportunities to reinforce his development by giving him related tasks.

There are various styles that can be adopted in delegating.

The best style is asking / coaching style where she is trying to develop him. But if she is in a hurry or the deadline is urgent she may adopt a telling / directing style where she simply tells him what to do. The latter is less risky and less time-consuming.

The two of them may over time develop a good working relationship where they agree which is most appropriate to the situation in hand (emergency = tell; less demanding timeframe = coaching).

Delegation is a useful **developmental tool** for increasing an employee's skill set if it is followed by feedback (as with the nurse above).

A Model For Feedback

Equally there is much management theory about the giving of feedback. One popular model is **BOOST** which stands for Balanced, Objective, Observed, Specific and Timely.

- Balanced means setting the bad in the context of the good – sometimes called a 'praise sandwich' (good / bad / good).
- Objective means that feedback should be based on behaviour, not personality ('You were late today' not 'You've got a slack attitude about getting to work on time'). This is because there's no point in criticising someone because of *who they are* (which they can't change). It's *what they do* that feedback is meant to try to change.
- Observed means that comments should be based on behaviour that has actually been observed, and not on hearsay.
- Specific means that comments are restricted to one particular item (more than one can be overload).
- Timely means that feedback is provided as soon after the behaviour in question as possible.

Training, Coaching And Mentoring

You can see that a lot of this is about developing team members, through **training** (formal courses usually provided by the function called Learning & Development), **mentoring** (a more senior person providing you with advice) and **coaching** (where the coach helps you by asking you questions that make you focus on what you are doing and how you are doing it, rather than telling you herself).

Role Play, Forum Theatre And Facilitation

Training methods these days include **role play** (participants take part in a real-life office situation where other members of staff can be played by actors) and **forum theatre** where the trainer will get participants to take it in turns to not only say what they would do in a certain situation but actually do it.

A lot of training these days is done through **facilitation**, where a group of people will discuss an issue and possible ways of addressing it while the facilitator keeps the discussion going and ensures that everyone has a chance to contribute, and where participants go into small **break-out groups** to **brainstorm** possible ways of addressing an issue or a situation then come back together in a **plenary** session to share their ideas.

Sometimes these training days take place away from the office and are called **retreats** or **off-sites**.

The Psychological Contract

A Harvard Business School professor called **Alfie Kohn** has written that the deal between employer and employee (he calls it the **psychological contract**) has changed.

It used to be: (employer) 'Give me your time and I will give you (employee) a job for life and a pension after it'. Now it is: (employee) 'I will lend you my skills for a period provided that during that time you (employer) develop my **skill set** further so that I can get a better role elsewhere'.

The challenge for employers is to provide such good learning and development, mentoring and coaching that even as they make their employees more marketable, those employees recognise that there isn't a better place to work.

For this reason learning no longer stops when you leave college. In order to remain in employment all your life in a fast-changing world you have to make sure that your skills remain relevant to the market and for that you need **lifelong learning**.

You will also need to develop your **time management** skills so that you work effectively, your **business writing** and **communication skills** so that your written work is concise, error-free and to the point, and your **presentation skills** so that you feel comfortable standing up and addressing a group.

Personality Types

The other big theme in the workplace is **team working**. Increasingly employees are asked to identify their **personality types** through systems such as Myers-Briggs Type Indicator (known as MBTI). This helps you know the sort of worker you are and the same about your colleagues, so you start to adjust to each other's way of working.

This is increasingly the case as the issues that organisations face become more complex, more multi-functional and, as organisations become more international, touch on offices in different countries and therefore different cultures.

Portfolio Working And Remote Working

Given what I said earlier about outsourcing and offshoring, organisations no longer offer jobs-for-life. For their part, more people are working part-time or flexible hours to cope with childcare and other duties. Some become **portfolio workers** and have a variety of part-time roles for different organisations.

Even full-time employees are increasingly working remotely (outside the office, for instance from home) and this makes it more challenging still to keep employees fully engaged and part of a team.

CHAPTER 10

WHAT ALL OF THIS MEANS FOR YOU

Client-facing – reliability – initiative – loyalty – open questions – closed question – EARS – interested

So why am I telling you all of this? Well, let's look at what we've covered so far: what business is and why; the importance of customers and markets; the impact of competitors; the need for strategy; the role of money in oiling the engine of business and providing fuel to expand; how businesses are organised and why; what people do in them; the importance of team working and learning and development.

What Commercial Awareness Is

Given everything we've covered, I think it's time for us to define what commercial awareness is.

I think it's this: understanding the role that you play in your organisation; who your clients or customers are and what matters to them; and how your role helps them.

The 'commercial' is understanding what business is about; the 'awareness' is understanding the purpose of your role.

All organisations have customers or clients. But not everyone in an organisation is **client-facing** – not everyone deals directly with the organisation's customers. Yet everyone has their own customer, a person they need to please. When you are junior that person is your boss, your manager.

Your job is to help them in their job. So you need to understand what they are doing and why, and why they need you to do your role.

Everyone in an organisation plays a valuable role otherwise the organisation wouldn't be paying to have that person on board. When the American space programme was in full swing in the 1960s, someone cleaning the floor at NASA (the space programme mentioned earlier) would have told you that they were helping to put a man on the moon. You don't put a man on the moon directly by cleaning floors. But unless the place is clean, dirt gets into the machinery and the rocket won't work.

Applying For Your First Job: Why Do They Need You?

So this is what I would do if I were applying for my first job.

I would find out everything I can about the organisation.

- I would look at its website and look online for where it has been mentioned in the media.
- I would try to find out what its mission is (does it have a slogan, for instance) and its history – do the people who established it still work in it?
- I would look for an organogram showing its structure.

- Above all I would ask what sector it's in and who its customers are. What is happening in that sector? How is it changing? What are the competitive pressures? Who are the big players?
- If I were the CEO what issues would keep me awake at night? What strategies would I be adopting?
- Ask yourself what an organisation's service, product or purpose is.

Then I would think about the specific role I am applying for.

- Which bit of the business will I be in?
- Who will my boss be? Who is his boss?
- What is his role? What does he need to do to be successful at it?
- Why is he looking to recruit someone to fill the role I am applying for?
- Why does he need that job done? How will it help him?
- If someone did that job well, what would it look like? If someone did it badly?
- If I were him what would I be looking for in someone like me? What qualities would he value the most? What experience?

These are all the questions that the organisation is asking about its customers. Your boss will be your customer, that's why you need to ask these questions.

Above all you need to be asking: why does the organisation need someone in this role? There must be a reason. People cost money so organisations don't recruit unless they have a commercial reason for doing so. Why do they need the additional resource that you'd represent? What is it they need you to do and why?

How This Will Help You

How will this help you? Two ways.

- First it will take you outside yourself and help you see yourself through the organisation's eyes – it will help you focus on what matters to them, not what matters to you.
- Second, it will arm you with lots of intelligent questions to ask which will show the boss that you have thought about the role, its purpose, how it helps him and how it helps the organisation.

Let's look first at what an organisation wants from someone like you. Young professionals going for jobs these days say they want prospects, promotion and responsibility. But a boss will respond: *How can you have prospects when you can't actually do anything valuable yet? Why should I consider promoting you when you can't even do the role I'm trying to fill? As for responsibility, do you know what that really means?*

A boss may even go on to say: *Management isn't about telling people what to do. If it was, anyone could do it. It's about dealing with issues and challenges. It's about taking difficult and complex decisions which are often risky and may upset people. It means taking the flak when one of your team does something incredibly stupid. It means taking it upon yourself to find a solution to a crisis when nobody knows what to do.*

Now, I know this doesn't sound very fair. But where does it leave you?

What Your Boss Wants From You

Since your boss is your first client and your job is to make his life easier, what does he want from you? What is he looking for? I think three things:

- Your boss wants **reliability**: someone who comes to work on time, all the time, who looks the part by dressing appropriately and neatly, who does all aspects of a task when asked, who does it on time and without fault and keeps him informed.

- He wants **initiative**: someone who can be given a piece of work and see it through, who can exhaust all aspects of it before saying it's done, who can see why they have been asked to do it and what a useful outcome looks like, who asks sensible questions and gets on with it, who knows when they have reached the limits of their knowledge and doesn't take risks or do anything stupid or irresponsible, and who will seize opportunities to develop their skills.

- Your boss wants **loyalty**: someone who will stick around, who won't keep asking for pay rises all the time, who will repay the faith shown when they were taken on by staying for at least 2-3 years before moving on, who puts the interests of the organisation and their boss before their own, who becomes a trusted lieutenant, who shows they are grateful for having been given a job. Your boss is looking out for stars of the future but right now the job is key.

Asking Questions

Now let's move on to questions about the role, what your boss wants, and the organisation. By asking questions it means you will have an actual discussion – he will ask you questions about yourself but you can ask him questions about the organisation and what matters to him about the role you are applying for.

To do this, use **open questions**. An open question is one which begins with a word like How or What or Why or Where or When. It is 'open' because it allows the other person to fashion a reply in whatever style and to whatever length they like. It opens them up.

A **closed question** is a direct question implying a yes or no answer. 'Do you feel OK?' is a closed question. 'How are you feeling?' is an open question. Closed questions are necessary sometimes, for instance to check your own understanding of what someone has said. Open questions are good when starting to get to know people. There's a helpful acronym called **EARS**:

- **E** – Engage: look people in the eye, smile, nod, to show them that they are getting through to you.
- **A** – Ask: use questions (see above).
- **R** – Reaffirm: this is about checking understanding: 'So am I right in thinking from what you've said that .....?'
- **S** – Silence: once you've asked a question, allow people time to think and respond; don't try to fill the space.

By the way, as the maxim has it, God gave you two ears and one mouth: use them in that proportion.

Be Interested Not Interesting

By asking questions you sound **interested** and that's what people want. Remember those evenings where someone you're with goes on and on – usually talking about themselves? Unless you were on a date together it may have seemed pretty boring to you. But to them it was a great time. What about those evenings that you think went pretty well and were really enjoyable? How much talking did you do? The key in professional life is to be interested not interesting. Ask questions rather than talk at people.

So you can ask questions that show you have looked into the organisation even if you don't know everything about it.

- You can ask about its strategy, the current business challenges, where it is seeking to innovate.
- And then you can set your boss's function in that context: the bit of the organisation where you'd be working – what is its role in relation to the organisation's strategy and challenges? What are the issues your boss is grappling with?
- And then that leads naturally on to your own role – if you were taken on by the business, how could you help your boss meet these challenges?

What Not To Say

Try not to make the mistake that a lot of young people do of saying 'I can improve your business' or 'I see my role as helping you achieve your strategy'. Your first few jobs in business will be junior while you learn something useful. If I were you I would be modest in my aspirations.

I would say that I am keen to learn how to do a job well. That is, after all, what you are being hired to do. There is a role that needs filling by someone who can do it well with the minimum of fuss and supervision. You want to learn how to do the job well; in return you want your skill set to be honed and expanded. I would ask about the training the organisation offers and how that would help me in the role.

Someone who pursues this line of questioning, who develops this discussion, shows me two things:

- They are interested in the organisation while realising their own role will be quite a small component in the achievement of its commercial objectives.
- But (second) they can see a connection between what they would be doing and my concerns and those of the organisation.

In other words they can see, however indirectly, how their role will help me in mine and relate it to the organisation. They are interested in those things without getting their own contribution out of proportion. In short they see how what they do is relevant in the wider context.

And that, you see, is what commercial awareness is: understanding your role in the wider context of your boss's role and the overall objectives and strategy of the organisation (even though in your first job your positive impact within the organisation will necessarily be limited). Commercial awareness is understanding how the product or service your organisation offers helps its customers in the wider context of their own objectives and goals (in a B2B context, their own strategy).

FINAL THOUGHTS

COMMERCIAL AWARENESS: AN ATTITUDE OF MIND

Once upon a time I worked for a book and magazine publisher. This was long before the internet, long before anything was online or available through ebook readers.

My boss, the CEO, was always asking bizarre questions. Once we were driving to a meeting and stopped at a traffic light. It was outside a bathroom showroom with showers in the window. 'Are more people taking showers than having baths, these days?' he asked. I had no idea. On another occasion (same car, different meeting) he overtook a cyclist. 'Are more people cycling to work than taking the tube, bus or train?' he asked (this was in London). Again, no idea.

Gradually I realised what he was doing. He was looking ahead.

If more people started taking showers instead of baths, fewer people would read our products in the bath. If people cycled to work they wouldn't read our products on their journey as they would on the tube, bus or train.

He was forever asking himself how the world was changing and our consumers with it. And as the world changed he made sure the company anticipated those changes so it wasn't caught out.

Attitude Of Mind

That's why, ultimately, commercial awareness is an attitude of mind, but one you can develop. It's about being interested in the commercial world around us. After all, these innovations which businesses develop and introduce are all designed to appeal to us, to make our lives easier or more enjoyable or more rewarding or safer or more comfortable.

People who are senior in their organisations care passionately about them and are thinking about them all the time.

If you can show that you are thinking about the purpose of your role and what it contributes, you are well on your way to becoming a useful employee and beginning to move up the ladder.

Once you show you are reliable, have initiative and are loyal, you will start to be promoted. But be patient and it will come. Be too demanding too early and you will be regarded as a pain. Show-offs may seem to get what they want sooner than anyone else. But solid, quiet application and hard work are never overlooked and are always rewarded in the end. Those are the people who become popular amongst their colleagues.

And this is the last thing I want to say about the world of work. Work is really important. There will be times in your life when other things are – your first significant relationship, setting up home, having children, and so on. But the backbone that will help link it all together is work.

I am often asked how to remain commercially aware. I hope you can see now that it's a mindset. It's about being interested in the world around you and how it works, and maintaining that air of wonder.

These days I live on a boat: I know, more or less, how a diesel engine works; but when my boat starts it's still a source of wonder to me. As I said at the start, when I go round supermarkets looking at the fantastic range of products on offer, I often pick them up just to inspect the label and see where they are from and wonder about how they got here. We are lucky to live in an amazing world.

In practical terms it's about remaining up-to-date with business trends and innovations – for instance through reading the financial pages of the newspapers, or something like *The Economist* which is a weekly magazine and contains short, incisive pieces on the latest developments in business and finance internationally. And whenever you meet somebody interesting from the business, commercial or financial worlds (or government for that matter), quizzing them about what they do and the issues their organisation faces.

It's the end of this book but the beginning of your career. All this book has done is to scratch the surface. It has given you some of the language of the commercial world and told you a bit about how it is organised and what matters to it so that you can ask sensible questions and understand at least some of the answers you'll get in reply. All I can do now is push you off in your boat and wish you the very best of luck.

Post Script

I said at the start of this book that the business that published the previous edition owed me a lot in royalties. So I terminated the contract and recovered the commercial rights to my books so I could publish them myself.

I knew I would never get those royalties back. But it so happened that what I was owed was exactly half of what my books earned in a year. So I consoled myself that I had effectively bought them back at a price/earnings of just a half.

Now you know what p/e ratios are you can see how good a deal that is and why – when it came to commercial awareness – I did in fact have the last laugh. Ciao.

The following index also serves as a glossary. Turn to the page where a term is first mentioned and that should be where its meaning is given.

INDEX / GLOSSARY